Creating with African Wax Fabric

Sew 20 Bold Projects
Sizes 2 to 24W

MARION COSTAMAGNA

stash BOOKS®

an imprint of C&T Publishing

Contents

Introduction

WHAT ARE AFRICAN WAX PRINTS?

A Little History

African wax prints are cotton fabrics that have been waxed on both sides, giving them hydrophobic properties. Colored waxes are used to create a wide variety of patterns. In Africa, they even represent a real language. The origin of African wax prints dates back to the nineteenth century during the colonial period, when Dutch colonists took inspiration from Indonesian batiks and began creating original and highly colorful patterns. When the Ghanaian soldiers who fought for the Dutch colony in Indonesia returned home, they brought back those fabrics that had captured their compatriots' hearts. Europeans saw this as an opportunity to trade peacefully with the African peoples and embark on the production of wax prints. Today, wax prints are still manufactured in the Netherlands and exported mainly to Africa. This fabric is increasingly sought after in Europe and on other continents.

Specifics of African Wax Prints

Be aware that the width of wax prints is generally smaller than that of other fabrics, ranging from 100cm to 120cm (39⅜in to 47¼in). Keep width in mind both when buying fabric and when positioning your pattern pieces. In this book, the pattern-cutting lines were made for fabric that is 110cm (43⅜in) wide.

VESTIAIRE'S 5 COMMANDMENTS

First Stop: The Laundry Room!

We understand you're eager to get started, but don't skip prewashing and ironing your fabric. There's a good reason: A lot of fabrics can shrink during the first wash. It would be a shame if you couldn't wear your masterpieces!

Iron Your Seams

We know ironing isn't anyone's idea of a great time. But what if we told you that this is the key to successful garment creation? After sewing the fabric, remember to spread open your allowances on both sides of the seam with the tip of your iron. Neat and tidy results, guaranteed!

Fusible Interfacing? What For?

Certain pieces, such as collars or waistbands, require interfacing to prevent them from distorting or wrinkling. Position the interfacing with the rough side against the wrong (non-printed) side of the fabric and iron the fabric (without steam). You may want to place some cotton fabric between your iron and the fabric so that the iron doesn't come into contact with the bonding adhesive.

Measuring Is a Sizable Step!

Bear in mind: Just because you wear a U.S. size 6 in ready-to-wear clothing or when you work with patterns from another designer, that doesn't necessarily mean you'll wear a size 6 in Vestiaire Éponyme patterns. So, before you start, get your precise measurements and refer to the sizing guide; this step is crucial for your creation's outcome. If you need help, you can always consult the measurement tips (next page).

When It Comes to Sewing, You Have to Be a Notch Above!

Remember to transfer the various marks with a small snip of the scissors (0.5cm / ³⁄₁₆in maximum) into your seam allowances. These notches will allow you to perfectly assemble your pieces for the best possible result!

ESSENTIAL EQUIPMENT

To be well prepared, you will need:

1. For making patterns after determining your size:
• tracing paper or special pattern paper,
• a pair of scissors for paper,
• a pencil, an eraser,
• a ruler, a square, French curves if you want to redesign and/or modify the patterns.
To reproduce the pattern pieces on paper, transfer them directly onto tracing paper or special pattern paper. Make sure to copy over every note and every mark as indicated on the patterns; then cut each piece.

2. For reproducing the patterns on the fabric and making the garments:
• tailor's chalk or a fine-tipped fabric marker,
• a pair of fabric scissors,
• an iron,
• a sewing machine with a zipper foot, a buttonhole foot, and a setting specifically for stretch fabric,
• standard needles and special needles for jersey, and thread for sewing cotton fabric,
• a box of pins,
• safety pins.
Once the pieces have been transferred onto paper, they must be reproduced on the fabric. To do this, follow the pattern layout to properly position the pieces so as not to waste too much fabric.
Be careful as well to position the pieces with the nap or pattern.
To keep the paper pieces from moving around on the fabric, you can hold them in place with weights, such as a book, notebook, or another heavy object.
If you're on the more daring side, you may cut the pieces directly. Alternatively, you can use chalk or a fabric marker to draw the outline of each piece on the fabric before cutting. Whichever you choose, make sure to **add the seam allowances, which are NOT included in the patterns.**

MEASUREMENT GUIDE

Each project has been designed for sizes 2 to 24, according to the following measurement table:

SIZE (U.S.)	BUST measurement	WAIST measurement	HIP measurement
2	80cm (31½in)	62cm (24½in)	86cm (33⅞in)
4	84cm (33⅛in)	66cm (26in)	90cm (35½in)
6	88cm (34¾in)	70cm (27⅝in)	94cm (37in)
8	92cm (36¼in)	74cm (29⅛in)	98cm (38⅝in)
10	96cm (37⅞in)	78cm (30¾in)	102cm (40¼in)
12	100cm (39⅜in)	82cm (3⅜in)	106cm (41¾in)
14	104cm (41in)	86cm (33⅞in)	110cm (43⅜in)
16	108cm (42½in)	90cm (35½in)	114cm (44⅞in)
18	112cm (44⅛in)	94cm (37in)	118cm (46½in)
20	116cm (45¾in)	98cm (38⅝in)	122cm (48⅛in)
22	120cm (47¼in)	102cm (40¼in)	126cm (49⅝in)
24	124cm (48⅞in)	106cm (41¾in)	130cm (51¼in)

Be sure to take your measurements before you try to determine your perfect size(s). If you are between sizes, don't hesitate to make a few adjustments to ensure the right fit of your garment!

How to Take Your Measurements
• Bust measurement
Measure your bust at its fullest point, loosely wrapping the tape horizontally around your body. For this measurement, wear your usual bra.
• Waist measurement
The waistline is measured at your thinnest point, often slightly above your navel. Stand up straight, legs hip-width apart, and don't suck your tummy in!
• Hip measurement
Measure your hips at the fullest point of your buttocks. Be sure to keep your tape measure horizontal.

READING THE INSTRUCTIONS

R/R, for "right against right," means that the "right" sides of your fabric should face each other. The back of your fabric should therefore be facing you when you sew.

Wrong side of the fabric

Right side of the fabric

When the assembly illustration is colored gray, it corresponds to the wrong (non-printed) side of the fabric.

When the assembly illustration is colored white, it corresponds to the right (printed) side of the fabric.

Throughout these projects, you will come upon different difficulty levels that involve mastering certain techniques:

Level 1: No problem! For these projects, you will usually only have to sew using the straight stitch. No risk of headache.

Level 2: Without any particular difficulty, these projects may be just right for eager beginners. They often involve mastering the simple straight stitch and hand sewing in a lining.

Level 3: For these projects, you will need to master adding zippers (invisible or otherwise) and sometimes work with more pieces or thicker layers.

Level 4: In addition to Level 3 techniques, these projects are generally more complex in their design and finish, as well as in the amount of fabric you will be working with.

Level 5: These projects often combine a lot of different techniques: adding zippers, gathering large quantities of fabric, working with many different pieces and layers, and even performing mental gymnastics during assembly.

Vestiaire Éponyme

Vestiaire Éponyme is a new sewing-pattern brand rooted in the pleasure of creation and the desire to rethink how we consume fashion. Marion, creator of Vestiaire Éponyme, is self-taught and obtained her education as she sewed. Today, after years of practice and experience, she offers her own designs and creations that are adaptable to your body type and your wishes, whatever they may be, and she's not afraid to break with tradition and blend styles.

Today, Vestiaire Éponyme celebrates African wax fabrics (Mondial Tissus) through elegant, contemporary pieces.

Did you say "Vestiaire Éponyme"?

Vestiaire Éponyme—that seems like a name that didn't just come out of nowhere. But then what's the story behind it? Marion explains ...

Vestiaire ?

"I chose the word Vestiaire ('wardrobe' or 'locker room' in English) for several reasons. The first, obviously, is because this word refers to that place where we store our clothes, the very ones we create, our 'cousettes' as we like to call them. But also because a locker room is a place of exchange and inspiration. That place where the team and the community gather around a common passion. It's a place where there is sharing, exchange, and the competitive drive, and that is the essence of my Vestiaire!"

And Éponyme ?

"Literally, éponyme ('eponymous') refers to something that bears the name of its creator, and in my opinion, this wardrobe is above all yours. The one you create, the one you wear, the one you present. Even if you're making something designed by someone else, it is your work, you are the creator, you are the boss, and in the end: it is your Vestiaire."

4 pieces

1
The Caroline *Skirt*

Caroline is a skirt that hugs your skin.
Fitted and with a small slit over the right leg,
it flaunts what it should with style.

Necessary Materials
For sizes 16 & 24
- 120cm (1¼yds) of fabric (110cm/43⅜in width) • 25cm (9⅞in) zipper in navy blue
- Fusible interfacing to reinforce waistband

SEAM ALLOWANCES
Seam allowances are not included. You will need to add 1cm (⅜in) on all sides of your pieces, with 2cm (⅞in) at the bottom for the hem. Note: These 2cm (⅞in) are essential for the best possible final product.

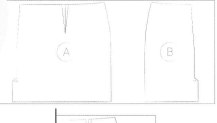

Cutting Layout

PATTERN
To access the pattern pieces through the QR code below, open the camera app on your phone, aim the camera at the QR code, and click the link that pops up on the screen.

To access the pattern through the tiny url, type the web address provided into your browser window.
tinyurl.com/11518-pattern1-download

ASSEMBLING THE FRONT OF THE SKIRT

1 - Make the dart Form the dart in the front section (A). To do this, bring the dart lines together R/R. Stitch on the wrong side of the fabric along the dart line. At the tip, do not stop, but continue a few more stitches off the fabric; then tie a knot to reinforce the dart closure. Iron down the inside of the dart.

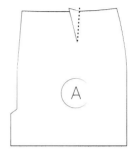

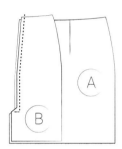

2 - Assemble the front pieces Place the two front pieces (A and B) R/R. Pin and stitch 1cm (⅜in) from the edge, stopping at the mark where the slit begins. Iron the seams open.

3 - Make the slit To make this easier, it's important to transfer all marks with chalk. Draw the hem fold: Mark 2cm (⅞in) from the bottom of the skirt (a, in green). Draw the slit line (b, in green), as well as the two angle bisectors, as shown opposite (c, in yellow, and d, in pink).

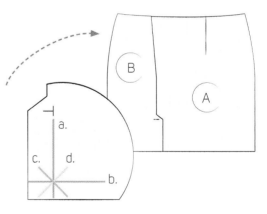

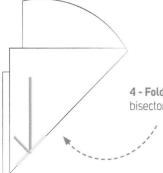

4 - Fold the slit R/R by lining up the hemline (a) and the slit line (b) so that the bisector (d) is on the fold.

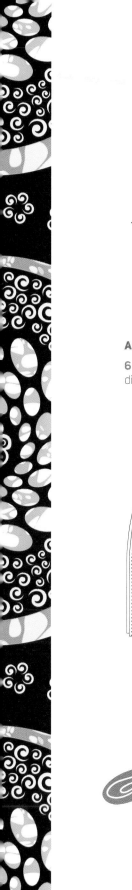

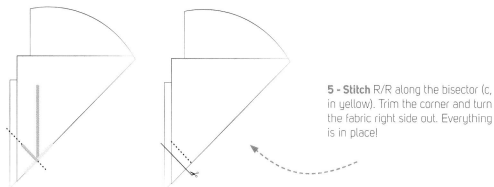

5 - Stitch R/R along the bisector (c, in yellow). Trim the corner and turn the fabric right side out. Everything is in place!

ASSEMBLING THE BACK

6 - Make the back darts Form the darts on each back section (piece C), just as you did with the front.

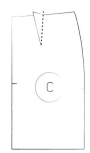

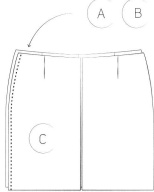

7 - Place the back and front sections R/R; then pin them along the sides. Stitch 1cm (⅜in) from the edge. Iron the seams open.

ASSEMBLING THE WAISTBAND

Before you start, remember to apply the interfacing to the wrong side of the exterior waistband.

We will call "D" the exterior waistband and "D'" the interior waistband (which can be made of a "lining" fabric).

8 - Attach the waistband Position the waistband (D) on the waistline of the skirt, edge to edge and R/R, making sure to match up the various seams and notches. Stitch 1cm (⅜in) from the edge all the way around.

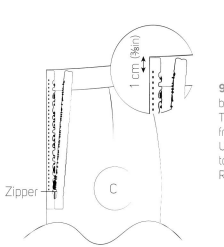

Zipper

9 - Attach the zipper Position the zipper R/R on one of the back pieces (C) of the skirt.

The plastic part at the top of the zipper should be 1cm (⅜in) from the top of the waistband.

Use the special zipper foot. Sew with a straight stitch as close to the teeth as possible until you reach the stopping notch. Repeat on the other side.

10 - Attach the interior waistband Position the interior waistband (D') on the exterior waistband (D) of the skirt, edge to edge and R/R, making sure to match the various notches. Stitch 1cm (⅜in) from the edge all the way around. Make sure the zipper is folded into the right side of the skirt.

11 - Pin the short edges of the waistband pieces (D and D')
R/R along the zipper. Stitch along the zipper.
Trim the corners and turn right side out.

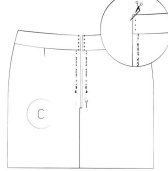

12 - Assemble the back Pin the two back pieces (C) and start your seam as close as
possible to the end of the zipper. Stitch, and then iron the seams open.

MAKING THE HEM

13 - Finish by hemming the bottom of the skirt.
To make your hem, start from the slit, where the
hem is naturally formed. Pin and stitch the entire
bottom of the skirt.

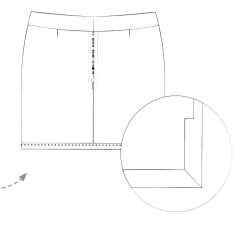

2 The Coline *Skirt*

What we love about Coline is the double-sided fabric, which gives volume and energy to this little skirt. Let your imagination run wild to find your personal combination of colors and materials!

Necessary Materials

For a size 16

• 150cm (1⅝yds) of fabric A (110cm/43⅜in width) • 55cm (⅝yd) of fabric B (110cm/43⅜in width) (to have underside of ruffle in another material) • 20cm (7⅞in) zipper in black • Fusible interfacing to reinforce waistband

For a size 24

• 120cm (1¼yds) of fabric A (110cm/43⅜in width) • 55cm (⅝yd) of fabric B (110cm/43⅜in width) (to have underside of ruffle in another material) • 55cm (⅝yd) of lining (110cm/43⅜in width)
• 20cm (7⅞in) zipper in black • Fusible interfacing to reinforce waistband

SEAM ALLOWANCES
Seam allowances are not included. You will need to add 1cm (⅜in) on all sides of your pieces.

Cutting Layout

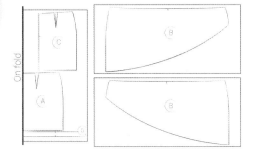

On fold

PATTERN

To access the pattern pieces through the QR code below, open the camera app on your phone, aim the camera at the QR code, and click the link that pops up on the screen.

To access the pattern through the tiny url, type the web address provided into your browser window.
tinyurl.com/11518-pattern2-download

Before starting, apply interfacing to the waistband piece (D) on the wrong side of the fabric.

Be careful not to use fabric that is too thick for the lining part of your ruffle piece (B) so that there aren't excessive layers of fabric.

ASSEMBLING THE FRONT OF THE SKIRT

1 - Make the darts Form the darts in the front piece (A). To do this, bring the dart lines together R/R.

Stitch on the wrong side of the fabric along the dart line. At the tip, do not stop, but continue a few more stitches off the fabric; then tie a knot to reinforce the dart closure.

Iron down the inside of the darts.

2 - Make the front panel Place the two B pieces R/R and stitch 1cm (⅜in) from the rounded edge.

Iron your seams open and turn the fabric right side out; then correctly match up the B pieces. You may want to use your iron to really flatten your pieces.

3 - Pin the remaining edges wrong sides together, and stitch 5mm (³⁄₁₆in) from the edge to keep them in place.

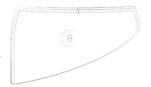

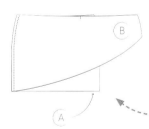

4 - Assemble the front Position piece B on the front piece (A) by lining up the long edge of the panel with the side of the skirt. The outside of the skirt and the "reverse side" (the part made in fabric B) of the panel should be facing you.

5 - Fold the panel at the notch (center of the panel), so that the short edge of the panel lines up with the side of your skirt.

Pin the side of the skirt (making sure that the waistlines of both the skirt and panel line up correctly). Stitch 7mm (⅓in) from the edge.

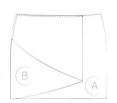

ASSEMBLING THE BACK OF THE SKIRT

6 - Make the darts Form the darts on each back piece (C), just as you did with the front.

7 - Position the zipper R/R on one of the back pieces (C) of the skirt. Make sure that the teeth of the zipper are on the right (printed) side, on the other side of the opening. The plastic part at the top of the zipper should be 1cm (⅜in) from the top of the skirt. Use the special zipper foot. Sew with a straight stitch as close to the teeth as possible until you reach the stopping notch. Repeat on the other side.

8 - Assemble the back Pin the two back pieces (C) and start your seam as close as possible to the end of the zipper.
Iron the seams open.

ASSEMBLING THE BACK AND FRONT

9 - Pin the front and back of the skirt together R/R along the sides and stitch 1cm (⅜in) from the edge.
Make sure to include every layer of the "panel" section. Iron the seams open.

ATTACHING THE WAISTBAND FACING

Before starting, apply interfacing to the waistband.

10 - Assemble the waistband facing Pin the waistband to the top of the skirt R/R. Remember to fold the zipper over the top of the skirt (the teeth must be on the printed side, on the other side of the opening). The end of the waistband should line up with the edge of the zipper. On the front section, make sure to pin all the layers together (both skirt and panel). Stitch 1cm (⅜in) from the edge all the way around.

11 - Pin the short edge of the waistband R/R along the zipper. Stitch along the zipper. Trim the corners.

12 - Topstitch To hold the facing in place, either understitch (before turning the facing right side out) or topstitch on the right (printed) side of the skirt.

MAKING THE HEM

13 - Finish by making the hem at the bottom of the skirt. To make your hem, make a crease 5mm (³⁄₁₆in) from the bottom of the skirt with your iron. Then fold the fabric over a second time to 1.5cm (⅝in). Pin and stitch 1cm (⅜in) from the edge.

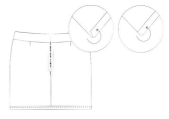

LEVEL 2/5

5 pieces

3

The Alizée *Skirt*

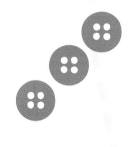

Alizée is a wrap skirt with a touch of madness: an asymmetrical cut, a large belt to tie, and a fully-lined finish!

Necessary Materials

For a size 16

• 130cm (1⅜yds) of fabric (110cm/43⅜in width) • 120cm (1¼yds) of fabric for lining (140cm/55⅛in width) • Fusible interfacing to reinforce waistband and button tab • 3 buttons, 20mm (¾in) in diameter maximum

For a size 24

• 130cm (1⅜yds) of fabric (110cm/43⅜in width) • 130cm (1⅜yds) of fabric for lining (140cm/55⅛in width) • Fusible interfacing to reinforce waistband and button tab • 3 buttons, 20mm (¾in) in diameter maximum

SEAM ALLOWANCES
Seam allowances are not included. You will need to add 1cm (⅜in) on all sides of your pieces.

Cutting Layout

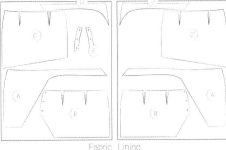

Fabric   Lining

PATTERN

To access the pattern pieces through the QR code below, open the camera app on your phone, aim the camera at the QR code, and click the link that pops up on the screen.

To access the pattern through the tiny url, type the web address provided into your browser window.
tinyurl.com/11518-pattern3-download

Instructions

Throughout these instructions, we will call the sections "A," "B," "C," and "D," and, when referring to the lining, "A'," "B'," "C'," and "D'." By the way, be sure to choose your lining carefully, because it will be visible on your finished work!

Note that since the skirt is asymmetrical, it will be necessary to reverse the direction of the lining pieces when cutting. If in doubt, place your fabric pieces on top of your lining to better understand the positioning of the pattern.

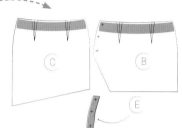

1 - Apply interfacing Before starting, apply interfacing to certain sections of your pieces (in dark gray, at right).

In particular, apply interfacing to the top of your B and C pieces at the waistband (a strip about 4cm/1⅝in wide), but also at the short edges of your B and B' pieces, where the buttons will be added.

Attach interfacing to the wrong side of your button tab pieces (E).

MAKING THE BELT

2 - Pin the belt pieces (D and D') R/R. Stitch 1cm (⅜in) from the edge all the way around, with the exception of the wide edge.

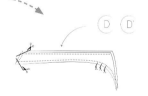

3 - Trim the corners, notch the rounded edge, iron the seams open, and turn right side out. Shape your belt, and iron to keep that shape in place.

ASSEMBLING THE FRONT OF THE SKIRT

4 - Make the darts Form the darts in piece B (this is the lower front part of the skirt). To do this, bring the dart lines together R/R. Stitch on the wrong side of the fabric along the dart line. At the tip, do not stop, but continue a few more stitches off the fabric; then tie a knot to reinforce the dart closure. Iron down the inside of the darts.

5 - Assemble the front and belt Place the previously assembled belt (D) on top of the front lower piece (B), lining up the sides. Make sure that the top of the belt is positioned just below the notch at the top of piece B. Stitch 5mm (³⁄₁₆in) from the edge to hold the belt in place.

6 - Make the darts Form the back darts (piece C), just as you did with the front.

ASSEMBLING THE SKIRT (EXTERIOR)

7 - Pin the front (B) and back (C) of the skirt, R/R, along the long side. Stitch 1cm (³⁄₈in) from the edge. Iron the seams open.

8 - Pin the front (A) and back (C) of the skirt, R/R, along the long side. Stitch 1cm (³⁄₈in) from the edge. Iron the seams open. The outside of your skirt is ready. Let's move on to the lining!

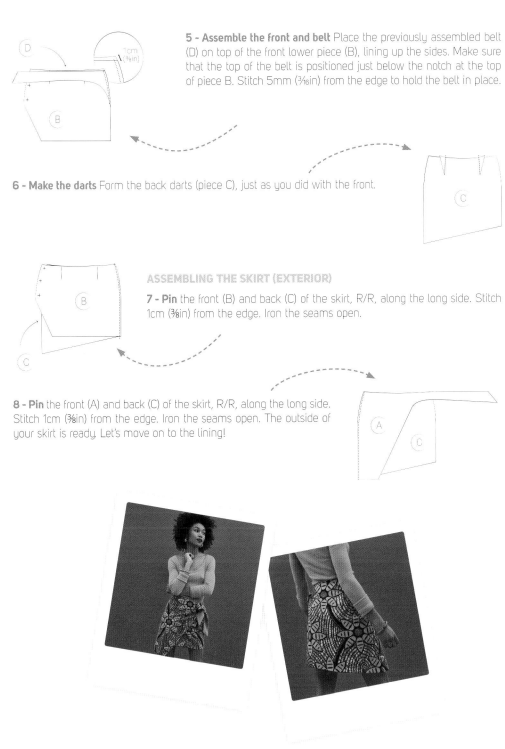

MAKING THE LINING

As a reminder, we refer to the pieces as "A," "B," and "C," and, when it comes to the "lining" pieces, "A'," "B'," and "C'."

9 - Make the button tab Pin the E pieces R/R and stitch 1cm (⅜in) from the edge along sides a, b, and c. Trim the corners, iron the seams apart, and turn right side out. Iron the button tab so that it's the right shape.

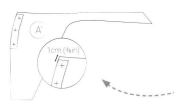

10 - Pin the (E) piece you just made to the A' piece R/R along the longer side, making sure that the top of the button tab is positioned 1cm (⅜in) below the top of A'.
Stitch 5mm (³⁄₁₆in) from the edge.

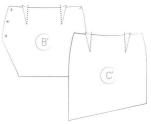

11 - Make the darts Form the darts in the front (B') and back (C') lining sections of the skirt.

ASSEMBLING THE LINING

12 - Pin the front (B') and back (C'), R/R, along the long side. Stitch 1cm (⅜in) from the edge. Iron the seams open.

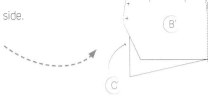

13 - Pin the front (A') and back (C'), R/R, along the long side. The button tab (E) should be sandwiched between A' and C'. Stitch 1cm (⅜in) from the edge. Iron the seams open.

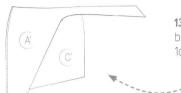

ASSEMBLING THE SKIRT

14 - Pin the skirt and lining, R/R, all the way around. Be careful to keep the belt clear of the skirt's edge so that it does not inadvertently get caught in the seam. Sew 1cm (⅜in) from the edge, leaving at least a 10cm (4in) opening in the bottom edge of the skirt.
Trim the various corners (skirt bottom, belt). Iron the seams open.
Turn right side out and shape the skirt with your iron.
Hand-stitch the opening closed.

FINISHING TOUCHES

All that's left is sewing in the interior buttons so you can fasten the skirt from the inside. To do this, place the buttons on the marks from the pattern. You can choose simple snap fasteners or make buttonholes in B and attach the buttons to E.

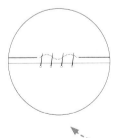

15 - Make the buttonhole Mark the buttonhole on piece B. To do this, simply place the buttons in the desired places and make two dots with a pencil or an erasable marker to mark the ends of the button (top and bottom). Remove the button and connect the two dots.

16 - Use this line to sew your buttonhole. Each sewing machine is different, but the settings are similar, so please refer to your machine's user manual or watch an online tutorial to help you visually with this step.

LEVEL 2/5

5 pieces

4
The Mélanie
Skirt

With its A-line cut and inverted pleats, the Mélanie skirt can be worn for any occasion and in any season. Perfect with heels, sneakers, or sandals, it works with everyone's style and body type!

Necessary Materials

For a size 16

• 130cm (1⅜yds) of fabric (110cm/43⅜in width) • Fusible interfacing for waistband
• 20cm (7⅞in) zipper in black

For a size 24

• 140cm (1½yds) of fabric (110cm/43⅜in width) • Fusible interfacing for waistband
• 20cm (7⅞in) zipper in black

Cutting Layouts

SEAM ALLOWANCES
Seam allowances are not included. You will need to add 1cm (⅜in) on all sides of your pieces.

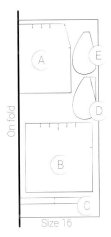

Size 16

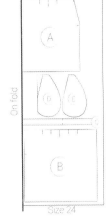

Size 24

PATTERN

To access the pattern pieces through the QR code below, open the camera app on your phone, aim the camera at the QR code, and click the link that pops up on the screen.

To access the pattern through the tiny url, type the web address provided into your browser window.
tinyurl.com/11518-pattern4-download

Instructions

MAKING THE PLEATS

1 - Front pleats Form the pleats in the front piece (A).
To do this, bring mark a and mark b together (toward the middle of your skirt). The notches should overlap, with the central notch (the longest on the pattern) positioned at the fabric fold.

2 - Pin and stitch 5mm (³⁄₁₆in) from the edge. Repeat with the other pleat in piece A.

3 - Back pleats For the back, you will have to create two pleats in each back piece (B). Do just as before by first lining up notch a1 with b, or by bringing the fabric back toward the "side" of the skirt. Then bring a2 and b together (this time, we bring the fabric back toward the "middle" of the skirt). Pin to hold the pleats in place, and stitch 5mm (³⁄₁₆in) from the edge.

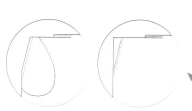

THE POCKETS

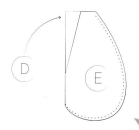

4 - Make the pockets Place the pocket lining (D) on the small pocket lining (E) R/R. Pin the rounded edge and stitch 1cm (³⁄₈in) from the edge. Repeat for both pockets.

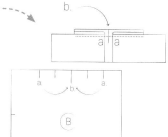

5 - Position the pockets Pin the small pocket lining (E) to the front of the skirt (A), edge to edge and R/R. Use the notches to get them in the right place. Stitch 1cm (³⁄₈in) from the edge and iron the seams open. To keep the pockets in place, you may want to topstitch the pocket opening (make sure you include only the front of the skirt [A] and the small pocket lining [E]).

6 - Turn the pockets into the inside of the skirt and pin them to the top and side of the skirt (A). Stitch 5mm (³⁄₁₆in) from the edge to hold them in place.

ASSEMBLING THE FRONT AND BACK OF THE SKIRT

7 - Pin the front and back of the skirt, edge to edge and R/R, along the sides. Stitch 1cm (³⁄₈in) from the edge. Iron the seams open.

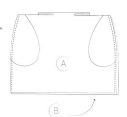

ATTACHING THE WAISTBAND

Before starting, apply interfacing to the exterior waistband on the wrong side of the fabric.
We will call the exterior waistband "C" and the interior waistband "C'" (which can be made of a "lining" fabric).

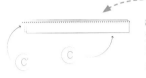

8 - Pin the two waistband pieces (C and C'), R/R, along the long edge. Stitch 1cm (⅜in) from the edge. To ensure the waistband is securely in place, topstitch the C seam on the facing side (C'). Shape the waistband using your iron.

9 - Place the exterior waistband (C), edge to edge and R/R, on the skirt, matching the notches on the side seams. Stitch 1cm (⅜in) from the edge.

ATTACHING THE ZIPPER

10 - Position the zipper R/R on one of the back pieces (B) of the skirt. Make sure that the teeth of the zipper are on the right (printed) side, on the other side of the opening. The plastic part at the top of the zipper should be at the fold of the waistband between C and C'. Use the special zipper foot. Sew with a straight stitch as close to the teeth as possible until you reach the stopping notch. Repeat on the other side.

11 - Pin the short edge of the waistband R/R along the zipper. Stitch along the zipper. Trim the corners and turn right side out. Use your iron to properly shape the waistband.

12 - To finish the waistband, you can either sew on the wrong side of the interior waistband (C') with an invisible stitch (by hand), or, on the right side, make a topstitch as close as possible to the edge of the waistband (C).

ASSEMBLING THE BACK

13 - Pin the two back pieces (C) and start your seam as close as possible to the end of the zipper. Iron the seams open.

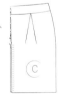

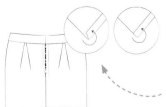

MAKING THE HEM

14 - Finish by making the hem at the bottom of the skirt. To make your hem, use your iron to crease 1cm (⅜in) from the bottom of the skirt. Fold the bottom of the skirt another 1.5cm (⅝in) (enclosing the first fold). Pin and stitch 1cm (⅜in) from the edge.

5 pieces

5
The Jérémie
Shorts

These simple short-shorts have attention to detail: piping at the pockets, pleats for a slight balloon look, and an exposed zipper on the back.

Necessary Materials
For sizes 16 & 24
• 100cm (1yd) of fabric (110cm/43⅜ width) • Fusible interfacing for waistband
• 50cm (19¾in) of piping (optional) • 20cm (7⅞in) zipper in ecru

SEAM
ALLOWANCES
Seam allowances are
not included. You will
need to add 1cm (⅜in)
on all sides of your
pieces.

Cutting Layout

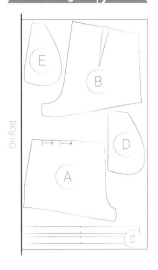

On fold

PATTERN
To access the pattern pieces through
the QR code below, open the camera
app on your phone, aim the camera
at the QR code, and click the link that
pops up on the screen.

To access the pattern through the tiny
url, type the web address provided into
your browser window.
tinyurl.com/11518-pattern5-download

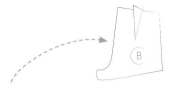

MAKING THE DARTS AND PLEATS

1 - Make the darts Form the darts on the back pieces (B) of the shorts. To do this, bring the dart lines together R/R. Stitch on the wrong side of the fabric along the dart line. At the tip, do not stop, but continue a few more stitches off the fabric; then tie a knot to reinforce the dart closure. Iron down the inside of the darts.

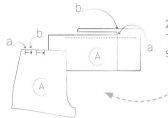

2 - Make the pleats Form the pleats on the front pieces (A) of the shorts. To do this, line up the notches in the direction of the arrows. Pin and stitch 5mm (³⁄₁₆in) from the edge to hold the pleats in place.

THE POCKETS

3 - Make the pockets Place the pocket lining (D) on the small pocket lining (E) R/R. Pin the rounded edge, and stitch 1cm (³⁄₈in) from the edge. Repeat for both pockets.

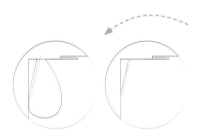

4 - Position the pockets Pin the small pocket lining (E) to the front of the skirt (A), edge to edge and R/R. If you so choose, this is where you can insert some pretty piping between the two pieces to highlight your pockets. Stitch 1cm (³⁄₈in) from the edge (and as close as possible to the piping allowance) and iron the seams open. To keep the pockets in place, you may want to topstitch the pocket opening (make sure you only include the front of the shorts [A] and the small pocket lining [E]).

5 - Turn the pockets into the inside of the shorts, and pin them to the top and sides of the shorts (A). Stitch 5mm (³⁄₁₆in) from the edge to hold them in place.

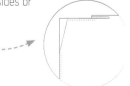

ASSEMBLING THE FRONT AND BACK

6 - Pin the front pieces (A) R/R; then sew them together from the crotch using a reinforced stitch.

7 - Pin the back pieces (B) to the previously assembled front section, R/R, along the sides. Stitch 1cm (³⁄₈in) from the edge and iron the seams open.

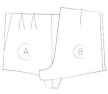

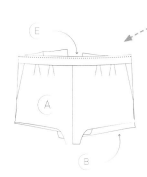

MAKING AND ATTACHING THE WAISTBAND

8 - Before starting, apply interfacing to the exterior waistband. We will call "C" the exterior waistband and "C'" the interior waistband (which can be made of a "lining" fabric).

Position the exterior waistband (C), edge to edge and R/R, on the shorts, matching up the notches and side seams. Stitch 1cm (⅜in) from the edge. Iron the seams open.

ATTACHING THE ZIPPER

9 - Position the zipper R/R on the back opening of the shorts. Make sure that the teeth of the zipper are on the right (printed) side, on the other side of the opening. The plastic part at the top of the zipper should be 1cm (⅜in) from the top of the waistband. Use the special zipper foot. Sew with a straight stitch as close to the teeth as possible until you reach the stopping notch. Repeat on the other side.

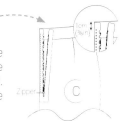

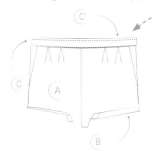

10 - Pin the interior waistband (C') to the exterior waistband (C), R/R, along the long edge. Stitch 1cm (⅜in) from the edge.

11 - Pin the short edge of the waistband R/R along the zipper. Stitch along the zipper. Trim the corners and turn the fabric right side out. Use your iron to properly shape the waistband.

12 - Sew a nice topstitch on the right (printed) side of the shorts to keep the waistband in place.

13 - Pin the two back pieces (B), and start your seam as close as possible to the end of the zipper. Iron the seams open.

ASSEMBLING THE LEGS

14 - Assemble front and back, R/R, from the crotch; then stitch 1cm (⅜in) from the edge using a reinforced seam. Iron the seams open.

MAKING THE HEM

15 - Finish by hemming the bottom of the legs. Working on the wrong side with your iron, make a crease 0.5cm (³⁄₁₆in) wide all the way around the leg hole. Fold another 1cm (⅜in) (enclosing the first fold). Pin and stitch 0.8cm (⅓in) from the edge to create a very thin hem.

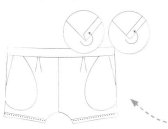

LEVEL 3/5

4 pieces

6
The Pascale
Top

Pascale, the simple and effective crop top. Wear with jeans or a high-waisted skirt for a cool, casual outfit.

Necessary Materials
For a size 16
- 120cm (1¼yds) of fabric (110cm/43⅜in width)

For a size 24
- 120cm (1¼yds) of fabric (110cm/43⅜in width) • 70cm (¾yd) of lining (110cm/43⅜in width)

SEAM ALLOWANCES
Seam allowances are not included. You will need to add 1cm (⅜in) on all sides of your pieces.

Cutting Layout

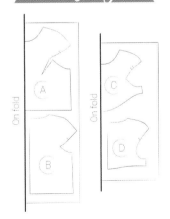

PATTERN

To access the pattern pieces through the QR code below, open the camera app on your phone, aim the camera at the QR code, and click the link that pops up on the screen.

To access the pattern through the tiny url, type the web address provided into your browser window.
tinyurl.com/11518-pattern6-download

MAKING THE DARTS

1 - On the front piece (A), form the darts in the armhole. To do this, bring the dart lines together R/R. Stitch on the wrong side of the fabric along the dart line. At the tip, do not stop, but continue a few more stitches off the fabric; then tie a knot to reinforce the dart closure. Iron down the inside of the darts.

ASSEMBLING BACK AND FRONT

2 - Place the front piece (A) on the back pieces (B), edge to edge and R/R, lining up the shoulder line and side edges.
Pin and stitch 1cm (⅜in) from the edge. Iron the seams open.

ASSEMBLING AND ATTACHING THE FACINGS

3 - Place the front facing (C) on the back facing (D), edge to edge and R/R, at the shoulder line. Pin and stitch 1cm (⅜in) from the edge. Iron the seams open.

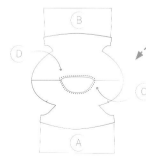

4 - Neckline Position the facing and the "exterior" pieces you've already assembled, edge to edge and R/R, at the neckline. To properly position the facing, be sure to match up the shoulder seams. Pin and stitch 1cm (⅜in) from the edge. Iron the seams open.

ASSEMBLING THE BACK

5 - Close the back (B). To do this, layer the pieces R/R, unfolding the facing pieces (D) upward so that they, too, can be positioned R/R. Pin and stitch 1cm (⅜in) from the edge. Iron the seams open.

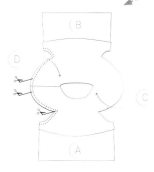

6 - Armholes Reposition the facing and "exterior" fabric pieces R/R and pin them at the armholes. Use the notches to properly position the facing. Stitch 1cm (⅜in) from the edge. At the armhole dart, be sure to stitch into the last stitch of the dart. Notch the corner of the armhole as well as the rounded edges of the cap sleeves before turning right side out and shaping the sleeve with your iron.

7 - Topstitching To keep the facing in place, you can stitch 1cm (⅜in) from the edge all the way around the neckline and armholes.

ASSEMBLING THE SIDES

8 - Position the front (A) and back (B) pieces, R/R, lining up the sides. Unfold the facing sections upward so that they, too, can be positioned R/R. Pin and stitch 1cm (⅜in) from the edge. Iron the seams open.

MAKING THE HEM

9 - Finish the top by hemming the bottom.
To make your hem, use your iron to crease 1cm (⅜in) from the bottom of the top.
Fold the bottom another 1.5cm (⅝in) (enclosing the first fold). Pin and stitch 1cm (⅜in) from the edge.

LEVEL 2/5

3 pieces

7
The Lisa
Top

Lisa is a sexy but classy top, with a plunging neckline in the back, nicely tied with a detailed ribbon. And the icing on the cake: Lisa is completely reversible, for a two-in-one top!

Necessary Materials

For a size 16
- Option 1: 120cm (1¼yds) (110cm/43⅜in width) if top is made with same fabric on both sides
- Option 2: 100cm (1yd) (110cm/43⅜in width) for outer fabric, 100cm (1yd) (110cm/43⅜in width) for lining fabric

For a size 24
- Option 1: 140cm (1½yds) (110cm/43⅜in width) if top is made with same fabric on both sides
- Option 2: 120cm (1¼yds) (110cm/43⅜in width) for outer fabric, 120cm (1¼yds) (110cm/43⅜in width) for lining fabric

SEAM ALLOWANCES
Seam allowances are not included. You will need to add 1cm (⅜in) on all sides of your pieces.

Cutting Layout

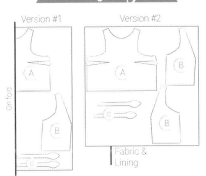

Version #1

On fold

A

B

C

Version #2

A

B

C

B

Fabric & Lining

PATTERN
To access the pattern pieces through the QR code below, open the camera app on your phone, aim the camera at the QR code, and click the link that pops up on the screen.

To access the pattern through the tiny url, type the web address provided into your browser window.
tinyurl.com/11518-pattern7-download

Instructions

What makes this top special is that it is fully reversible, so choose your lining well and have fun combining the fabrics!

Throughout the explanations, we will call the sections "A," "B," and "C"; and, when referring to the lining, "A'," "B'," and "C'."

MAKING THE DARTS

1 - Form the darts in front piece (A) and lining (A').

To do this, bring the dart lines together R/R.

Stitch on the wrong side of the fabric along the dart line. At the tip, do not stop, but continue a few more stitches off the fabric; then tie a knot to reinforce the dart closure. Iron down the inside of the darts.

ASSEMBLING BACK AND FRONT

2 - Place the front piece (A) on the back pieces (B), edge to edge and R/R, at the shoulder line. Pin and stitch 1cm (⅜in) from the edge. Iron the seams open. Repeat with the A' and B' pieces.

3 - Pin the front and back pieces to their linings R/R at the neckline, up to the stopping notch in the back neckline. Stitch 1cm (⅜in) from the edge. Notch the rounded neckline before turning right side out; then iron the neckline.

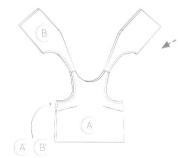

4 - Turn the lining inside out to reposition the exterior fabric and lining R/R; then pin the pieces at the armholes, making sure to match the shoulder seams. As before, stitch 1cm (⅜in) from the edge and notch the rounded armhole. Do the same for the second sleeve.

Turn your garment right side out by sliding the back through the shoulders.

MAKING AND ATTACHING THE SASH

5 - Layer both C pieces R/R (one in "fabric," the other in "lining"). Pin and stitch 1cm (⅜in) from the edge all the way around the sash, with the exception of the short edge.
At the tip of the sash, leave the needle down, raise the presser foot, and rotate the fabric to position it in the right direction. Lower the pressure foot and continue sewing.
Notch the corner and turn right side out. Press the sash with your iron.
Do the same with the second sash.

ATTACHING THE SASH TO THE BODICE

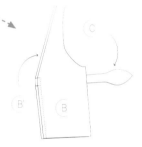

6 - Position the back pieces (B and B'), edge to edge and R/R, inserting one of the sashes in between (the fabric part [C] must be against B, and C' against B'). The sash should be positioned between the notches.
Pin all the way to the bottom of the top, and stitch 1cm (⅜in) from the edge. Iron the seams apart and turn right side out.
Repeat on the other side.

ASSEMBLING THE SIDES

7 - Place the front pieces (A) on the back pieces (B), edge to edge and R/R, matching the sides and unfolding the linings upward so that the front and back linings are also R/R. Be sure to match the armhole seams. Stitch 1cm (⅜in) from the edge. Iron the seams open. Do the same for both sides of the top.

FINISHING TOUCHES

8 - To finish the top, turn it inside out and position both fronts (A and A'), as well as both backs (B and B'), edge to edge and R/R. Pin and stitch 1cm (⅜in) from the edge all the way around, leaving a 10cm (4in) opening at the bottom of the top.

10cm (4in)

9 - Trim the various corners, and iron the seams open. Turn right side out using the 10cm (4in) opening, and shape the top with your iron.
Hand-stitch the small opening closed.

5 pieces

8

The Violette Top

What we love about Violette is its straight, unstructured cut, with playful ruffles and a delicate opening in the back.

Necessary Materials

For a size 16
• 130cm (1⅜yds) (110cm/43⅜in width) for main fabric • 40cm (½yd) (150cm/1⅝yds width) for ruffles* • 50cm (⅝yd) of ribbon for tie OR 1 button for button closure

For a size 24
• 160cm (1¾yds) (110cm/43⅜in width) for the main fabric • 80cm (1yd) (150cm/60in width) for the ruffles* • 50cm (⅝yd) of ribbon for tie OR 1 button for button closure

*Be aware that depending on the width of your fabric, you may have to cut 4 ruffle strips instead of 2 at the fold.

SEAM ALLOWANCES
Seam allowances are not included. You will need to add 1cm (⅜in) on all sides of your pieces.

Cutting Layouts

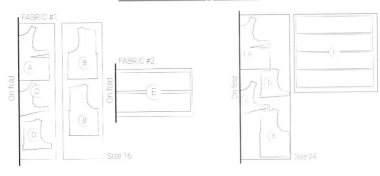

PATTERN
To access the pattern pieces through the QR code below, open the camera app on your phone, aim the camera at the QR code, and click the link that pops up on the screen.

To access the pattern through the tiny url, type the web address provided into your browser window.
tinyurl.com/11518-pattern8-download

Instructions

MAKING THE DARTS

1 - Form the darts in the front piece (A).
To do this, bring the dart lines together R/R.
Stitch on the wrong side of the fabric along the dart line. At the tip, do not stop, but continue a few more stitches off the fabric; then tie a knot to reinforce the dart closure. Iron down the inside of the darts.

ASSEMBLING BACK AND FRONT

2 - Place the front piece (A) on the back pieces (B), edge to edge and R/R, at the shoulder line. Pin and stitch 1cm (⅜in) from the edge. Iron the seams open.

3 - Position the front (C) and back (D) facings, edge to edge and R/R, at the shoulder line. Pin and stitch 1cm (⅜in) from the edge. Iron the seams open.

4 - Pin the previously assembled front (A) and back (B) pieces to their facings, R/R, at the neckline. Stitch 1cm (⅜in) from the edge. Notch the rounded neckline before turning right side out; then iron the neckline.

5 - Turn back inside out to reposition the fabric and facing R/R. Pin the pieces together at the armholes, making sure to match the shoulder seams using the notches. As before, stitch 1cm (⅜in) from the edge and notch the rounded armhole.
Do the same for the second sleeve.
Turn your garment right side out by sliding the back through the shoulders.

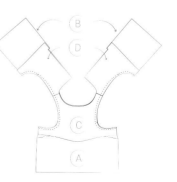

How to Make a Button Loop

There are different options for making your button loop. You may decide to:

1/ Make the button loop out of fabric by cutting a 2cm (⅞in)-wide rectangle with a length equal to the button diameter plus an additional 2.5cm (1in) (for ease of passage and seam allowance). For a 20mm (¾in)-diameter button, we would therefore have a button loop 2cm (⅞in) wide by 4.5cm (1¾in) long. Use your iron to create a 5mm (³⁄₁₆in) crease lengthwise on each side of your rectangle. Then fold the rectangle in half to get a rectangle 4.5cm (1¾in) long by about 5mm (³⁄₁₆in) wide. Your fabric button loop is ready.

2/ Use a small piece of elastic or a thin round cord (use the same method as above for calculating the length of the button loop).

3/ Embroider or braid your strap after it's been made (don't forget to add an additional 5mm (³⁄₁₆in) to let your button pass through easily).

6 - Assemble the back

Place the first back piece (B) on the facing (D), edge to edge and R/R. Before sewing, insert either a piece of ribbon about 20cm (7⅞in) long or a small button loop (see How to Make a Button Loop, above) between the two pieces at the notch near the back neckline. Pin and stitch 1cm (⅜in) from the edge.

When you get to the corner, leave the needle down, raise the presser foot, and rotate the fabric to position it in the right direction. Lower the presser foot and continue sewing to the edge. Iron the seams open.

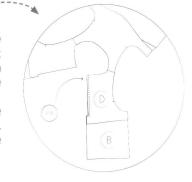

7 - Close the back Assemble the back pieces (B), edge to edge and R/R, unfolding the small facing pieces (D) upward so that they too can be positioned R/R. Pin and stitch 1cm (⅜in) from the edge. Iron the seams open.

8 - Assemble the sides Place the front (A) and back (B) edge to edge and R/R, unfolding the front (C) and back (D) facings upward so that they too can be positioned R/R. Pin and stitch 1cm (⅜in) from the edge. Iron the seams open.

MAKING THE RUFFLES

9 - Assemble the ruffles Position the ruffle strips (E) R/R. Pin them along one of the short edges and stitch 1cm (⅜in) from the edge. Iron the seam open.

10 - Hem the ruffles To do this, use your iron to make a 1cm (⅜in)-wide crease down the entire length of the ruffle strip. Fold the bottom of the strip another 1.5cm (⅝in) (enclosing the first fold). Pin and stitch 1cm (⅜in) from the edge.

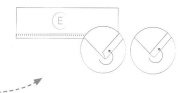

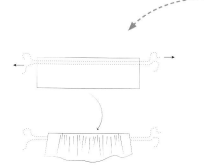

11 - Gather the fabric To create your ruffles, you will have to sew using a long straight stitch (set your stitch length to 4). Make your first line 0.5cm (³⁄₁₆in) from the edge without tying off at the start or finish. Leave at least 5cm (2in) of thread loose on each side. Sew a second line 1.5cm (⅝in) from the edge (1cm/⅜in further in than the first line) using the same technique as before.

Pull the two bobbin threads (alternating from one side of the piece to the other) to gather the fabric.

Do this until the length of the ruffles matches the length of the bottom of the top.

Once you have the right length, set the ruffles by knotting the ends of the threads.

12 - Attach the ruffles to the bodice Position the ruffle strips (E) R/R. Pin them along the remaining short edge and stitch 1cm (⅜in) from the edge. Iron the seam open.

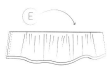

13 - Position the ruffles on the bottom of the top R/R. The ruffles should extend all the way around. Pin and stitch 1cm (⅜in) from the edge. Iron the seam down.

14 - Layered effect To create this effect, pinch the fabric 3cm (1¼in) above the seamline above the ruffles. Pull these 3cm (1¼in) of fabric to 3cm (1¼in) beneath the ruffles. Pin and stitch 3cm (1¼in) above the edge of this fold.

FINISHING TOUCHES

15 - To finish your top, attach the button on the back neckline (opposite the strap). Thoroughly iron your top!

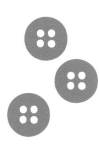

5 pieces

9 The Camille Top

With its asymmetrical cut, scooped neckline, and long sash, to tie in a bow or leave free, Camille just begs for the sun!

Necessary Materials
For sizes 16 & 24: 190cm (2yds) (110cm/43⅜in width)

SEAM ALLOWANCES
Seam allowances are not included. You will need to add 1cm (⅜in) on all sides of your pieces.

Cutting Layouts

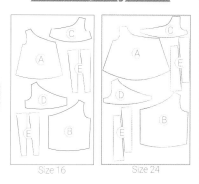

Size 16   Size 24

PATTERN
To access the pattern pieces through the QR code at right, open the camera app on your phone, aim the camera at the QR code, and click the link that pops up on the screen.

To access the pattern through the tiny url, type the web address provided into your browser window.
tinyurl.com/11518-pattern9-download

ASSEMBLING THE SASH

1 - Assemble the four sash pieces with the front (A), back (B), front facing (C), and back facing (D) R/R.

ASSEMBLING THE FRONT AND FACING

2 - Place the front facing (C) on the front piece (A), edge to edge and R/R. Pin along the entire neckline, down to the armholes, passing through the sash at the shoulder. Stitch 1cm (⅜in) from the edge. Notch the corners and rounded edges before turning right side out to form the front section. Do the same with the back piece (B) and the back facing (D).

ASSEMBLING THE FRONT AND BACK

3 - Place the front on the back, R/R, lining up the sides. Unfold the facing upward so that the front and back facings can be positioned R/R as well. Pin and stitch 1cm (⅜in) from the edge. Iron the seams open.

MAKING THE HEM

4 - Finish the top by making the hem. To do this, use your iron to make a 1cm (⅜in)-wide crease at the bottom of the top. Fold another 1.5cm (⅝in) (enclosing the first fold). Pin and stitch 1cm (⅜in) from the edge. Your top is now ready!

6 pieces

10 The Rémy *Pullover*

With its loose fit, puffy sleeves, and a bow at the waist, this is THE comfy pullover. Don't be scared to mix fabrics and materials to highlight the different sections.

Necessary Materials

For a size 16
• 80cm (⅞yd) (140cm/55⅛in width) for body • 30cm (⅓yd) (110cm/43⅜in width) for sleeves
• 50cm (⅝yd) of 1cm (⅜in)-wide elastic for sleeves

For a size 24
• 90cm (1yd) (140cm/55⅛in width) for body • 80cm (⅞yd) (110cm/43⅜in width) for sleeves
• 50cm (⅝yd) of 1cm (⅜in)-wide elastic for sleeves

Cutting Layouts

SEAM ALLOWANCES
Seam allowances are not included. You will need to add 1cm (⅜in) on all sides of your pieces.

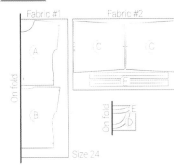

PATTERN

To access the pattern pieces through the QR code below, open the camera app on your phone, aim the camera at the QR code, and click the link that pops up on the screen.

To access the pattern through the tiny url, type the web address provided into your browser window.
tinyurl.com/11518-pattern10-download

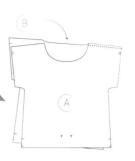

Instructions

Be aware that depending on the width of your fabric, you may have to cut the ribbon piece (F) twice instead of just once at the fold.

ASSEMBLING BACK AND FRONT

1 - Shoulder line Place the front piece (A) on the back piece (B), edge to edge and R/R, along the shoulder line. Pin and stitch 1cm (⅜in) from the edge. Iron the seams open.

2 - Neckline Place the ends of the front (D) and back (E) facings together, R/R. Pin, stitch 1cm (⅜in) from the edge, and iron the seams apart.

3 - Position the already assembled facing at the neck of the sweater, edge to edge and R/R. To properly position the facing, be sure to match the shoulder seams. Pin and stitch 1cm (⅜in) from the edge. Iron the seams open before folding the facing toward the inside of the pullover.

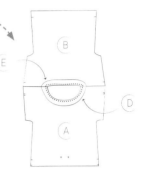

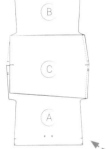

PREPARING AND ASSEMBLING THE SLEEVES

4 - Attach the sleeves to the body. Be sure to attach the "front" of the sleeves to the front of the pullover, and the "back" of the sleeves to the back of the pullover (follow the notches). Pin and stitch 1cm (⅜in) from the edge. Iron the seams open.

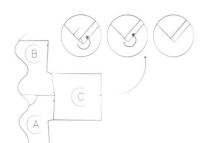

5 - At the cuff of the sleeve (where your hand will come out), you will need to make a double hem. To do this, use your iron to make a first fold of 1cm (⅜in), then a second of 2cm (⅞in). Pin and stitch 5mm (³⁄₁₆in) from the edge of the fold.

6 - Attach a safety pin to the end of the elastic and slide it into the resulting tube. Play with the fabric to move the safety pin through the tube.
When the other end (the one without the pin) is about to enter the tube, pin the elastic to the edge of the fabric and stitch 7mm (⅓in) from the edge with a reinforced stitch.
Continue to pull the safety pin through until the elastic reappears on the other side of the tube. Once this has happened, pin it to the edge of the fabric and stitch 7mm (⅓in) from the edge with a reinforced stitch.

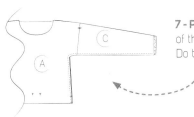

7 - Pin the underside of the sleeves R/R, as well as the front and back of the pullover. Stitch 1cm (⅜in) from the edge. Iron the seams open. Do the same for the second sleeve.

MAKING THE TIE AND BUTTONHOLE

8 - Make the tie Fold the strip (F) lengthwise and R/R. You may want to crease with your iron. Pin and stitch 1cm (⅜in) from the edge. 1cm (⅜in) before reaching the end, leave the needle down, raise the presser foot, rotate the fabric 90 degrees, lower the presser foot again, and continue sewing the small edge of the strip. Notch the corners. Iron the seams open and turn right side out.

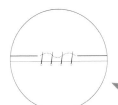

9 - At the unsewn end of the ribbon, pull the edges 1cm (⅜in) inward. Pin and hand sew an invisible stitch. Your tie is now ready.

10 - Make the buttonhole In order to pull the tie through the hem of the pullover, you'll need to make two buttonholes where indicated on the pattern. You may want to transfer the mark from the pattern (2.5cm/1in long) onto the fabric so you can refer to it when sewing the buttonhole. Each sewing machine is different, so please refer to your machine's user manual or watch an online tutorial to help you visually with this step.

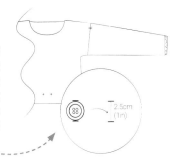

11 - Make the hem Your buttonholes are ready. You can now make the bottom hem of your pullover.
To do this, make a 1cm (⅜in) crease on the wrong side of the fabric using your iron. Then, still using the iron, make a new crease of 4cm (1⅝in), so that the notch is within the fold. Check that the buttonhole marks are in the center of the hem.
Pin this hem and stitch 5mm (³⁄₁₆in) from the edge.

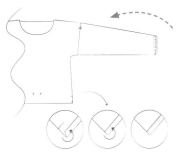

12 - Add the tie

Attach a safety pin to the end of the tie and slide it into the tube of the hem. Play with the fabric to move the safety pin through the tube until it comes out again. Make sure you don't lose sight of the other end (the side without the pin).

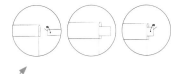

LEVEL
4/5

8 pieces

11

The Éva
Dress

Éva, what a knockout! A skater skirt with inverted pleats, a sash to tie at the shoulder, a neckline with a surprising back—it goes without saying that Éva will turn some heads.

Necessary Materials

For a size 16
• 390cm (4¼yds) of fabric (110cm/43⅜in width) • 40cm (15¾in) invisible zipper • One button, 20mm (¾in) in diameter maximum

For a size 24
• 450cm (5yds) of fabric (110cm/43⅜in width) • 40cm (15¾in) invisible zipper • One button, 20mm (¾in) in diameter maximum

Be aware that depending on the width of your fabric, you may have to cut two front pieces (F) instead of cutting just once at the fold.

PATTERN

To access the pattern pieces through the QR code below, open the camera app on your phone, aim the camera at the QR code, and click the link that pops up on the screen.

To access the pattern through the tiny url, type the web address provided into your browser window.
tinyurl.com/11518-pattern11-download

SEAM ALLOWANCES
Seam allowances are not included. You will need to add 1cm (⅜in) on all sides of your pieces.

Cutting Layout

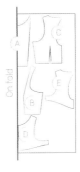

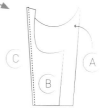

ASSEMBLING THE BODICE - FRONT

1 - Form the front by positioning pieces B on top of piece A. Pin and stitch 1cm (⅜in) from the edge. Iron the seams open.

MAKING THE BACK DARTS

2 - Form the darts in the back pieces (C). To do this, bring the dart lines together R/R. Stitch on the wrong side of the fabric along the dart line. At the tip, do not stop, but continue a few more stitches off the fabric; then tie a knot to reinforce the dart closure. Iron down the inside of the darts.

MAKING THE SHOULDER SASH

3 - Pin two of your "sash" pieces (H) R/R, and stitch all the way around, with the exception of one of the small edges. Trim the corners and turn the sash right side out via the small side left open.

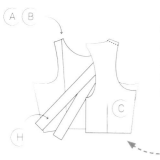

ASSEMBLING THE BODICE

4 - Assemble the front and back Place the previously assembled front piece onto the back pieces, edge to edge and R/R, at the shoulder line. On one of the shoulders, insert the two sashes (1cm /⅜in should remain on each side of the sashes). Stitch 1cm (⅜in) from the edge and iron the seams open.

ASSEMBLING THE FACINGS

5 - Shoulder line Place the front facing (D) on the back (E), edge to edge and R/R, at the shoulder line. Pin and stitch 1cm (⅜in) from the edge. Iron the seams open.

How to Make a Button Loop

There are different options for making your button loop:

1/ Make the button loop out of fabric by cutting a 2cm (⅞in)-wide rectangle with a length equal to the button diameter plus an additional 2.5cm (1in) (for ease of passage and seam allowance). For a 20mm (¾in)-diameter button, we would therefore have a button loop 2cm (⅞in) wide by 4.5cm (1¾in) long. Use your iron to create a 5mm (³⁄₁₆in) crease lengthwise on each side of your rectangle. Then fold the rectangle in half to get a rectangle 4.5cm (1¾in) long by about 5mm (³⁄₁₆in) wide. Your fabric button loop is ready.

2/ Use a small piece of elastic or a thin round cord (use the same method as above for calculating the length of the button loop).

3/ Embroider or braid your strap after it's been made (don't forget to add an additional 5mm (³⁄₁₆in) to let your button pass through easily).

6 - Neckline Pin the facing to the previously assembled bodice, R/R, at the neckline. Stitch 1cm (⅜in) from the edge. Be careful not to inadvertently sew into the shoulder sash. Notch the rounded neckline before turning right side out; then iron the neckline.

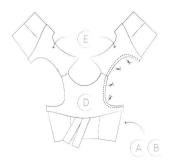

7 - Close the back Turn back inside out to position the back pieces (C) with their facings (E), edge to edge and R/R, at the back opening. On one side, insert the button loop into the small seam allowance. It should be on the inside of the top (sandwiched between the fabric and the facing). Pin and stitch 1cm (⅜in) from the edge, starting from the neckline toward the bottom of the "teardrop" opening. Trim the corners and notch the rounded edges before turning right side out to shape the piece with your iron.

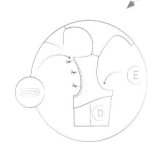

8 - Create the armholes Turn inside out to reposition the fabric and facing R/R. Pin the pieces at the armholes. Pin and stitch 1cm (⅜in) from the edge, taking care not to sew into the sash (for the shoulder in question).

Notch the rounded armhole. Turn your garment right side out by sliding the back through the shoulders.

ASSEMBLING THE SIDES

9 - Line up the front and back sides of your top, edge to edge and R/R, unfolding the facings upward so that they, too, can be positioned R/R. Pin and stitch 1cm (⅜in) from the edge. Iron the seams open. Repeat on the other side.

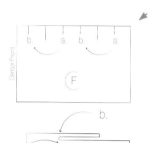

ASSEMBLING THE SKIRT

10 - Make the pleats To make the pleats, bring mark a and mark b together (toward the middle of the skirt). The notches should overlap, with the central notch (the longest on the pattern) located at the fold. Do the same for each pleat.

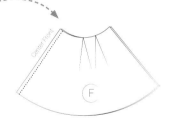

11 - Assemble the skirt front Be aware that depending on your size and the width of your fabric, you may have to cut piece (F) twice. If this is the case, first assemble the two front pieces (F) by placing them R/R, lined up with the middle of the skirt. Pin and stitch 1cm (⅜in) from the edge. Iron the seams open. Otherwise, proceed to the next step.

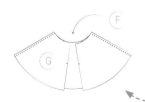

12 - Assemble the front and back of the skirt Pin the front and back of the skirt, R/R, along the sides. Stitch 1cm (⅜in) from the edge. Iron the seams open.

ASSEMBLING THE DRESS

13 - To assemble the bodice and skirt of the dress, place the bodice and skirt R/R, lined up at the waistline. Your bodice should be inside the skirt. Match the various side seams. Pin and stitch 1cm (⅜in) from the edge. Iron the seams open.

ATTACHING THE ZIPPER

14 - Position the zipper R/R along the back opening of the dress. Make sure that the teeth of the zipper are on the right (printed) side of the fabric, on the other side of the opening. The plastic part at the top of the zipper should be where the fabric and facing meet (C/E). To do this, unfold the back facing upward. Use the special invisible zipper foot. Sew with a straight stitch as close to the teeth as possible until you reach the stopping notch. Repeat on the other side.

15 - Fold the facing back over the fabric R/R so that the zipper is positioned between the two, the teeth facing the right (printed) side of the fabric. Stitch along the zipper until the bottom of the facing. Trim the corners and reposition the facing on the inside of the dress.

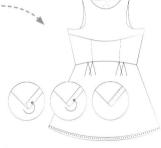

16 - Pin the bottom back of the dress and start your seam as close as possible to the end of the zipper.
Iron the seams open.

MAKING THE HEM

17 - Finish the dress by making the hem. To make your hem, use your iron to crease 1cm (⅜in) from the bottom of the dress.
Fold another 1.5cm (⅝in) (enclosing the first fold). Pin and stitch 1cm (⅜in) from the edge.

LEVEL 5/5

8 pieces

12
The Josette
Dress

Josette is a lightweight wrap dress with an underskirt and ruched cap sleeves to give it the volume and movement we love. Wear it anytime, anywhere!

Necessary Materials

For a size 16
- 220cm (2⅜yds) (110cm/43⅜in width) for bodice and its facings
- 150cm (1⅝yds) (140cm/55⅛in width) for pleated skirt

For a size 24
- 230cm (2½yds) (110cm/43⅜in width) for bodice and its facings
- 150cm (1⅝yds) (140cm/55⅛in width) for pleated skirt

SEAM ALLOWANCES
Seam allowances are not included. You will need to add 1cm (⅜in) on all sides of your pieces.

Cutting Layout

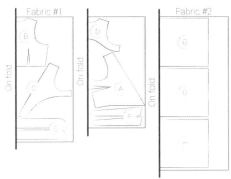

PATTERN
To access the pattern pieces through the QR code below, open the camera app on your phone, aim the camera at the QR code, and click the link that pops up on the screen.

To access the pattern through the tiny url, type the web address provided into your browser window.
tinyurl.com/11518-pattern12-download

MAKING THE SASHES

1 - Place two of the sash pieces (F) R/R. Pin and stitch 1cm (⅜in) from the edge all the way around, with the exception of the short edge. When you get to a corner of the sash, leave the needle down, raise the presser foot, and rotate the fabric to position it in the right direction. Lower the presser foot and continue sewing. Do the same with the second sash.

MAKING THE DARTS

2 - Form the darts in the front (A) and back (B) pieces. To do this, bring the dart lines together R/R. Stitch on the wrong side of the fabric along the dart line. At the tip, do not stop, but continue a few more stitches off the fabric, then tie a knot to reinforce the dart closure. Iron down the inside of the darts.

ASSEMBLING BACK AND FRONT

3 - Place the front pieces (A) on the back piece (B), edge to edge and R/R, at the shoulder line. Pin and stitch 1cm (⅜in) from the edge. Iron the seams open.

4 - Place the front (C) and back (D) facings, edge to edge and R/R, at the shoulder line. Pin and stitch 1cm (⅜in) from the edge. Iron the seams open.

5 - Pin the previously assembled front (A) and back (B) pieces with their facings, R/R, at the neckline. Be aware that you will need to sandwich the sash (F) (the one cut at an angle) between the facing and the fabric on one side of the front, 1cm (⅜in) above the bottom of the bodice (use the notches to properly position your sash). On the other side of the front, insert a piece of ribbon, about 20cm (7⅞in) long, in the same way. Stitch 1cm (⅜in) from the edge. Notch the rounded neckline before turning right side out, and then iron the neckline.

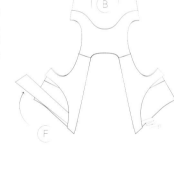

MAKING AND ASSEMBLING THE SLEEVES

6 - Prepare the sleeves Make a double hem on the outer edge of the sleeve by making a crease at 5mm (³⁄₁₆in), then a second at 1cm (⅜in) (enclosing the first fold). Pin and stitch 8mm (⅓in) from the edge.

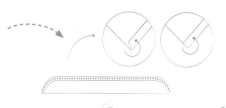

7 - Gather the inner edge of the sleeves

To do this, sew one line 0.5cm (³⁄₁₆in) from the edge without tying off at the start or finish. Leave at least 5cm (2in) of thread loose on each side. Sew a second line 1.5cm (⅝in) from the edge (1cm /⅜in further in than the first line) using the same technique as before. Pull the two bobbin threads (alternating from one side of the piece to the other) to gather the fabrics. Do this until the length of the ruffles matches the required length (use the notches on the armholes). Once you have the right length, set the ruffles by knotting the ends of the threads.

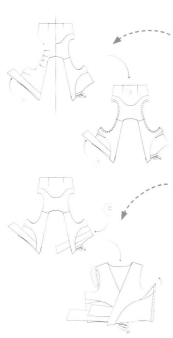

8 - Assemble the cap sleeves Turn the bodice back inside out to reposition the fabric and facing R/R. Pin the pieces at the armholes by inserting the sleeves between the facing and the fabric. To properly position these, use the notches. The right (printed) side of your sleeves should be against the right side of the bodice (and not the right side of the facing). Pin and stitch 1cm (⅜in) from the edge and notch the rounded armhole. Do the same for the second sleeve. Turn the bodice right side out using the tube formed by the shoulders.

ASSEMBLING THE SIDES

9 - Position the front pieces on the back of your bodice, edge to edge and R/R, unfolding the facings upward so that they, too, can be positioned R/R. On the opposite side to the one where the sash (F) is located, insert the second sash (F) (the one with the square edge). Pin and stitch 1cm (⅜in) from the edge. Iron the seams open. Repeat on the other side (without sash or ribbon inserted).

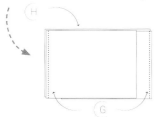

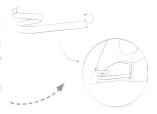

10 - Take a second piece of ribbon about 20cm (7⅞in) long. Depending on the material of your ribbon, burn the edge or make a small hem to prevent it from fraying. Position it on the inside of the bodice, at the side seam (side opposite the previously attached ribbon), 1.5cm (⅝in) above the waistline. Use the seam allowance to secure it. Stitch 0.8cm (⅓in) and 0.5cm (³⁄₁₆in) from the edge, in the seam allowance.

MAKING THE SKIRT

11 - Assemble back and front Assemble your back (H) and front (G) rectangles, R/R, from the sides. Stitch 1cm (⅜in) from the edge. Iron the seams open.

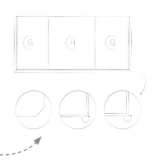

12 - Make the hem You will hem the sides and bottom of the skirt. To do this, use your iron to make a 1cm (⅜in)-wide crease down the entire length of the ruffle strip. Fold the bottom of the skirt another 1.5cm (⅝in) (enclosing the first fold). Pin and stitch 1cm (⅜in) from the edge. Do the same for all three sides. For beautifully finished corners, notch the corners at 5cm (2in).

13 - Gather the skirt To make your ruffles, sew with a long straight stitch (set your stitch length to 4). Make your first line 0.5cm (³⁄₁₆in) from the edge without tying off at the start or finish. Leave at least 5cm (2in) of thread loose on each side. Sew a second line 2cm (⅞in) from the edge (1cm /⅜in further in than the first line) using the same technique as before. Pull the two bobbin threads (alternating from one side of the piece to the other) to gather the fabric. Do this until the length of the ruffles matches the circumference of the bodice, making sure to match the seams. Once you have the right length, set the ruffles by knotting the ends of the threads.

ASSEMBLING THE DRESS

14 - Place the skirt and bodice, R/R, making sure to match the side seams of the bodice with those of the skirt. Pin and stitch 1cm (⅜in) from the edge. Be careful not to inadvertently sew the ribbons into the seam. Iron the seams open; then turn right side out.

13
The Émilie
Dress

6 pieces

LEVEL 1/5

Émilie is an A-line dress with a yoke at the bottom that will highlight your upper body thanks to its geometric cuts. A little bonus: Émilie has small pockets concealed in the seams.

Necessary Materials
For a size 16
• 80cm (⅞yd) (110cm/43⅜in width) for yoke • 120cm (1¼yds) (140cm/55⅛in width) for bodice
• Silver lurex piping

For a size 24
• 80cm (⅞yd) (110cm/43⅜in width) for yoke • 150cm (1⅝yds) (140cm/55⅛in width) for bodice
• Silver lurex piping

Cutting Layouts

SEAM ALLOWANCES
Seam allowances are not included. You will need to add 1cm (⅜in) on all sides of your pieces.

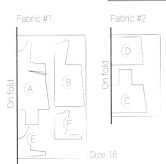

Size 16

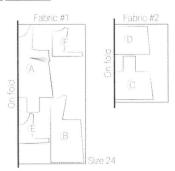

Size 24

PATTERN
To access the pattern pieces through the QR code below, open the camera app on your phone, aim the camera at the QR code, and click the link that pops up on the screen.

To access the pattern through the tiny url, type the web address provided into your browser window.
tinyurl.com/11518-pattern13-download

63

Instructions

MAKING THE DARTS

1 - On the front piece (A), form the darts. To do this, bring the dart lines together R/R. Stitch on the wrong side of the fabric along the dart line. At the tip, do not stop, but continue a few more stitches off the fabric; then tie a knot to reinforce the dart closure. Iron down the inside of the darts

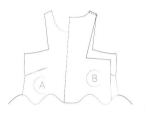

ASSEMBLE THE FABRIC

2 - Assemble the fabric Place your front (A) and back (B) pieces, edge to edge and R/R, at the shoulder line. Pin and stitch 1cm (⅜in) from the edge. Iron the seams open.

3 - Assemble the facing Place your front (E) and back (F) facing, edge to edge and R/R, at the shoulder line. Pin and stitch 1cm (⅜in) from the edge. Iron the seams open.

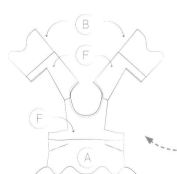

4 - Neckline Pin the previously assembled front (A) and back (B) pieces with their facings R/R at the neckline. Stitch 1cm (⅜in) from the edge. Notch the rounded neckline and corners before turning right side out and shaping the bodice with your iron.

5 - Armholes Turn back inside out to reposition the fabric and facing R/R. Pin your pieces at the armholes. As before, stitch 1cm (⅜in) from the edge and notch the rounded armhole. Do the same for the second armhole. Feed your pieces back through the sleeve tube to turn right side out.

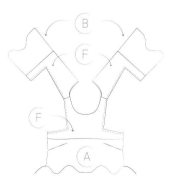

6 - Assemble the back Layer the two back pieces of the dress, edge to edge and R/R, unfolding the facings upward so that they, too, can be positioned R/R. Pin and stitch 1cm (⅜in) from the edge. Iron the seams open.

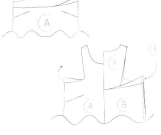

7 - Assemble the sides of the dress Place the sides of the front and back pieces edge to edge and R/R, again unfolding the facings upward so that they, too, can be positioned R/R. Pin and stitch 1cm (⅜in) from the edge. Iron the seams open. Repeat on the other side.

ASSEMBLING THE YOKE

8 - Place the front yoke (C) on the back yoke (D), R/R, and pin on each side. Stitch 1cm (⅜in) from the edge. Iron the seams open.

9 - Attach the yoke Slide the yoke over the bottom of the dress, R/R. The dress should be inside the yoke. Pin all the way around (including the pockets) and stitch 1cm (⅜in) from the edge. Iron the seams open and turn right side out. Using your iron, shape the yoke and pockets.

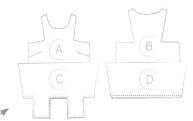

MAKING THE HEM

10 - Finish the dress by making the hem. To make your hem, use your iron to crease 1cm (⅜in) from the bottom of the dress. Fold another 1.5cm (⅝in) (enclosing the first fold). Pin and stitch 1cm (⅜in) from the edge.

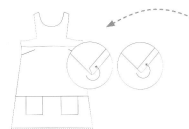

LEVEL 3/5

9 pieces

14
The Lucie
Dress

What we love about Lucie is the small batwing sleeves that bring volume and airiness to the silhouette.
The added bonus: Use the belt to add your personal style to the dress.
With or without, tied in a bow or left free, it's up to you!

Necessary Materials

For a size 16
• 145cm (1⅝yds) of fabric (140cm/55⅛in width) for bodice • 150cm (1⅝yds) of fabric (110cm/43⅜in width) for skirt and belt • 40cm (15¾in) invisible zipper in black

For a size 24
• 150cm (1⅝yds) of fabric (140cm/55⅛in width) for bodice • 190cm (2yds) of fabric (110cm/43⅜in width) for skirt and belt • 40cm (15¾in) invisible zipper in black

SEAM ALLOWANCES
Seam allowances are not included. You will need to add 1cm (⅜in) on all sides of your pieces.

Cutting Layouts

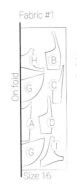

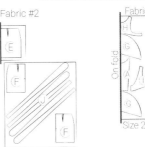

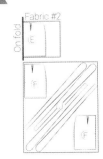

PATTERN
To access the pattern pieces through the QR code below, open the camera app on your phone, aim the camera at the QR code, and click the link that pops up on the screen.

To access the pattern through the tiny url, type the web address provided into your browser window.
tinyurl.com/11518-pattern14-download

Instructions

MAKING THE BODICE

1 - Prepare the sleeves Make a double hem on the rounded edge of the sleeve. To do this, use your iron to make a 5mm (³⁄₁₆in)-wide crease, then fold again 0.8cm (¹⁄₃in) (enclosing the first fold). Pin and stitch 5mm (³⁄₁₆in) from the edge. You can also make a rolled hem. However, depending on the thickness of the fabric, we do not recommend lining the sleeve, both for how the garment falls and because of an upcoming step where an oversized sleeve could be problematic!

2 - Assemble the bodice Position one front side piece (B) on one back side piece (D), R/R. Pin at the shoulder line, and stitch 1cm (³⁄₈in) from the edge. Iron the seam open. Repeat with the other side.

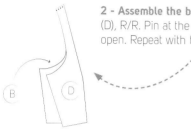

3 - Position the center front piece (A) and the center back piece (C), R/R. Pin at the shoulder line and stitch 1cm (³⁄₈in) from the edge. Iron the seam open.

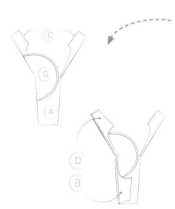

4 - Place one of the previously assembled "side" pieces on the "center" piece, R/R, sandwiching in the previously prepared sleeve. To properly position the sleeve, you may want to mark the middle of the sleeve to match with the shoulder seam. Also, the right (printed) side of the sleeve should be positioned against the right side of the "center" part. Pin and stitch 1cm (³⁄₈in) from the edge. Iron the seams open. Do the same for the second sleeve.

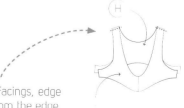

5 - Make and attach the facings Place the front (H) and back (I) facings, edge to edge and R/R, at the shoulder line. Pin and stitch 1cm (³⁄₈in) from the edge. Iron the seams open.

6 - Pin the facing to the previously assembled bodice, R/R, at the neckline. Stitch 1cm (⅜in) from the edge. Be careful not to inadvertently sew into the ruffled sleeve. Notch the rounded neckline before turning right side out; then iron the neckline.

7 - Turn back inside out to reposition the fabric and facing R/R. Pin the pieces together at the armholes, making sure to match the shoulder seams. Your ruffled sleeves should be sandwiched between the pieces and kept clear of the seamline so they're not inadvertently sewn into. Stitch 1cm (⅜in) from the edge. Notch the rounded armhole, iron the seams open, and turn right side out via the shoulder tube. Do the same for the second sleeve.

8 - Assemble the sides Line up the front and back sides of the bodice, edge to edge and R/R, unfolding the front and back facings upward so that they, too, can be positioned R/R. Pin and stitch 1cm (⅜in) from the edge. Iron the seams open. Repeat on the other side.

MAKING THE SKIRT

9 - Make the darts Form the darts on the front (E) and back (F) pieces of the skirt. To do this, bring the dart lines together R/R. Stitch on the wrong side of the fabric along the dart line. At the tip, do not stop, but continue a few more stitches off the fabric; then tie a knot to reinforce the dart closure. Iron down the inside of the darts.

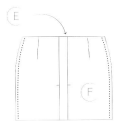

10 - Assemble the skirt at the sides Pin the front and back of the skirt R/R. Assemble at the sides and stitch 1cm (⅜in) from the edge. Iron the seams open.

ASSEMBLING THE DRESS

11 - To assemble the bodice and skirt of the dress, position the bottom of the bodice and the top of the skirt R/R, making sure to match the various seams (darts and side seams). Pin and stitch 1cm (⅜in) from the edge. Iron the seams open.

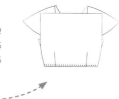

ATTACHING THE ZIPPER

12 - Position the zipper R/R along the back opening of the dress. Make sure that the teeth of the zipper are on the right (printed) side, on the other side of the opening. The plastic part at the top of the zipper should be where the exterior fabric and facing meet (C/I). To do this, unfold the back facing upward. Use the special zipper foot. Sew with a straight stitch as close to the teeth as possible until you reach the stopping notch. Repeat on the other side.

13 - Fold the facing back over the fabric R/R so that the zipper is positioned between the two, the teeth facing the right side of the fabric. Stitch along the zipper until the bottom of the facing. Trim the corners and reposition the facing on the inside of the dress.

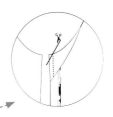

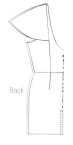

14 - Pin the bottom back of the skirt and start your seam as close as possible to the end of the zipper.
Iron the seams open.

Back

MAKING THE HEM

15 - Finish the dress by making the hem. To make your hem, use your iron to crease 1cm (⅜in) from the bottom of the dress.
Fold another 1.5cm (⅝in) (enclosing the first fold). Pin and stitch 1cm (⅜in) from the edge.

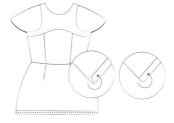

MAKING THE BELT (REMOVABLE)

16 - Place the J pieces R/R and stitch 1cm (⅜in) from the edge along the small edge.

17 - Place the previously formed belt pieces (J) R/R and stitch all the way around 1cm (⅜in) from the edge, leaving an opening of 10cm (4in). Notch the rounded areas.

18 - Turn right side out via the 10cm (4in) opening. Pin the opening and hand sew it closed with an invisible stitch. All that's left is tying the belt around your waist!

71

15
The Anonymous
Dress

Imagine that with only 3 strips of fabric, you could wear infinite dresses.
This is the promise of the Anonymous Dress.
Let your desires and imagination run free as you wrap the straps around
your body, and imagine YOUR one-of-a-kind dress.

Necessary Materials

For a size 16
• 280cm (3yds) of fabric (110cm/43⅜in width) • Some fusible interfacing to reinforce waistband
• 25cm (9⅞in) zipper

For a size 24
• 480cm (5¼yds) of fabric folded on cross grain (110cm/43⅜in width) • Some fusible interfacing
to reinforce waistband • 25cm (9⅞in) zipper

Cutting Layouts

SEAM ALLOWANCES
Seam allowances are not included. You will need to add 1cm (⅜in) on all sides of your pieces.

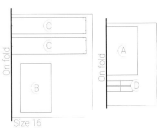

Size 16

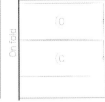

Size 24

PATTERN

To access the pattern pieces through the QR code below, open the camera app on your phone, aim the camera at the QR code, and click the link that pops up on the screen.

To access the pattern through the tiny url, type the web address provided into your browser window.
tinyurl.com/11518-pattern15-download

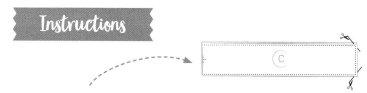

Instructions

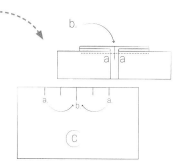

MAKING THE STRAPS

1 - Lined version If you have chosen to line your fabric, place two of your straps (C) R/R. Pin them and stitch 1cm (⅜in) from the edge, with the exception of one short edge. Notch the corners and turn right side out.

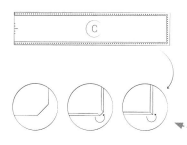

2 - Unlined version If you do not want to line your straps, make a double hem all the way around, with the exception of one short edge. For beautifully finished corners, notch the corners at 2.5cm (1in). Fold the cut corner 5mm (³⁄₁₆in) over the wrong side of the fabric. Iron the fold to keep it in place. Fold one of the sides first 5mm (³⁄₁₆in), then another 1cm (⅜in). Pin and stitch 8mm (⅓in) from the edge. Do the same for the other side of the corner. There must be no gap between the two hems. Do the same with the other corner.

3 - Make the pleats On the still "raw" strap (without hem or lining and still open), form the pleats. To do this, match the outer notches with the central notch (the longest on the pattern). Do the same for the second pleat in the strap. Pin and stitch 5mm (³⁄₁₆in) from the edge to hold the pleats in place. Do the same for the second strap.

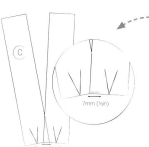

4 - Assemble the straps Put the two straps together by positioning them right side against wrong side, overlapping 3cm (1¼in) (at the "raw" edge). Pin and stitch 7mm (⅓in) from the edge to hold them in place.

ASSEMBLING THE STRAPS AND WAISTBAND

5 - Apply interfacing to the exterior waistband (the one that will be visible when the dress is worn). For the rest of the instructions, we will call (D) and (D') the exterior and interior waistbands respectively. Position the exterior waistband (D) and the previously assembled straps R/R. The center front of the waistband and the center of the shoulder straps should line up. Place the exterior waistband (D) and interior waistband (D') R/R (so that the straps are sandwiched between the waistband panels). Pin and stitch 1cm (⅜in) from the edge. Iron the seams open and turn right side out.

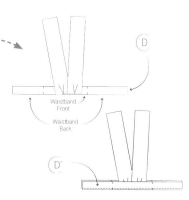

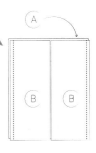

MAKING THE SKIRT

6 - Assemble the back and front Assemble your front (A) and back (B) rectangles R/R along the sides. Stitch 1cm (⅜in) from the edge. Iron the seams open.

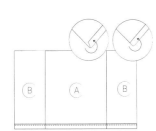

7 - Hemming Make the hem of the skirt. To do this, use your iron to make a 1cm (⅜in)-wide crease down the entire length of the ruffle strip. Fold the bottom of the skirt another 1.5cm (⅝in) (enclosing the first fold). Pin and stitch 1cm (⅜in) from the edge.

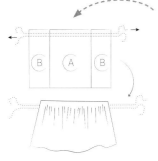

8 - Gather the fabric To make the ruffles, sew using a long straight stitch (set your stitch length to 4). Make your first line 0.5cm (⅜in) from the edge without tying off at the start or finish. Leave at least 5cm (2in) of thread loose on each side. Sew a second line 2cm (⅞in) from the edge (1cm /⅜in further in than the first line) using the same technique as before. Pull the two bobbin threads (alternating from one side of the piece to the other) to gather the fabrics. Do this until the length of the ruffles matches the length of the waistband. To distribute your ruffles correctly, match the side seams with the notches in the side of the waistband. Once you have the right length, set the ruffles by knotting the ends of the threads.

ASSEMBLING THE SKIRT

9 - Place your skirt and exterior waistband R/R, making sure to line up the side seams with the reference notches of your waistband. Pin (including the interior waistband) and stitch 1cm (⅜in) from the edge. Iron the seams open; then turn right side out.

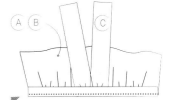

ATTACHING THE ZIPPER

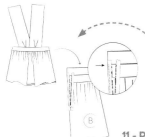

10 - Unfold the interior waistband (D') upward and place the zipper R/R on one of the back pieces by positioning the plastic part of your zipper at the fold between the exterior and interior waistbands. Make sure that the teeth of the zipper are on the right (printed) side, on the other side of the opening. Use the special zipper foot. Sew with a straight stitch as close to the teeth as possible. Repeat on the other side.

11 - Pin the short edge of the waistband R/R along the zipper. Stitch along the zipper. Trim the corners and turn right side out. Use the iron to properly shape your waistband.

12 - Close the rest of the dress by pinning the back R/R, and start your seam as close as possible to the end of the zipper. Iron the seams open.

13 - To finish the dress, topstitch on the right side as close as possible to the edge of the waistband (C).

16
The Gérard
Pants

Gérard: THE pants that will show off your figure. With a high waist, flared cut, and pretty belt, Gérard combines comfort and elegance.

Necessary Materials
For sizes 16 & 24
- 270cm (2⅞yds) (110cm/43⅜in width)
- Fusible interfacing to reinforce belt
- 22cm (8¾in) invisible zipper in navy blue

Cutting Layout

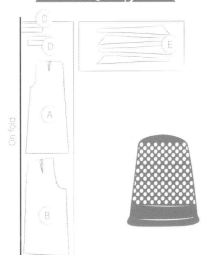

On fold

SEAM ALLOWANCES
Seam allowances are not included. You will need to add 1cm (⅜in) on all sides of your pieces.

PATTERN
To access the pattern pieces through the QR code below, open the camera app on your phone, aim the camera at the QR code, and click the link that pops up on the screen.

To access the pattern through the tiny url, type the web address provided into your browser window.
tinyurl.com/11518-pattern16-download

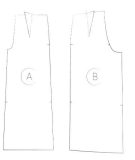

MAKING THE DARTS

1 - Form the darts in the front (A) and back (B) pieces of the pants. To do this, bring the dart lines together R/R. Stitch on the wrong side of the fabric along the dart line. At the tip, do not stop, but continue a few more stitches off the fabric; then tie a knot to reinforce the dart closure. Iron down the inside of the darts.

ASSEMBLING THE FRONT AND BACK

2 - Pin the front pieces (A) R/R; then assemble them from the crotch using a reinforced stitch.

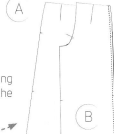

3 - Pin the back pieces (B) to the previously assembled front section, R/R, along the sides. Use the notches to properly position the pieces. Stitch 1cm (⅜in) from the edge and iron the seams open.

MAKING THE WAISTBAND

Before starting, apply interfacing to the front (C) and back (D) waistband pieces.

4 - Make the sashes Place two sash pieces R/R and stitch 1cm (⅜in) from the edge all the way around, with the exception of the shorter end (the one that will allow you to turn the sash right side out). Notch the corners and turn right side out; then iron to make it look nice. Do the same with the second sash.

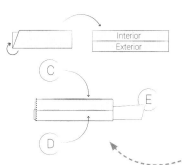

5 - Assemble the sashes Crease the front (C) and back (D) waistband pieces lengthwise. Decide on one of the sides to be the exterior waistband (visible when the pants are worn). Place the front waistband (C) and the back (E) R/R, sandwiching the sash in the "exterior" part of the waistband. The sash should be a good centimeter above the top edge of the waistband. Pin and stitch 1cm (⅜in) from the edge. Do the same at the other end of the waistband with the second sash.

ASSEMBLING THE WAISTBAND

6 - Place the waistband on top of the pants, edge to edge and R/R, making sure to match the various seams. Stitch 1cm (⅜in) from the edge all the way around.

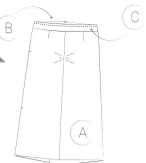

ATTACHING THE ZIPPER

7 - Position the zipper R/R over the back opening of the pants. Make sure that the teeth of the zipper are on the right (printed) side, on the other side of the opening. The plastic part at the top of the zipper should be at the fold between the exterior and interior waistbands. Use the special invisible zipper foot. Sew with a straight stitch as close to the teeth as possible until you reach the stopping notch. Do the same with the second back side.

8 - Pin the interior and exterior waistbands R/R along the short edge. Stitch along the zipper. Trim the corners, turn right side out, and use your iron to properly shape the waistband.

9 - Sew a nice topstitch on the pants to keep the waistband in place.

10 - Pin both back pieces (B), and start your seam as close as possible to the end of the zipper and to the base of the crotch. Iron the seams open.

ASSEMBLING THE LEGS

11 - Assemble the front and back, R/R, from the crotch; then stitch 1cm (⅜in) from the edge using a reinforced seam. Iron the seams open.

MAKING THE HEM

12 - Finish by making the hems at the bottom of the legs. Working on the wrong side with your iron, make a crease 1cm (⅜in) wide all the way around the leg hole. Fold another 1.5cm (⅝in) (enclosing the first fold). Pin and stitch 1cm (⅜in) from the edge.

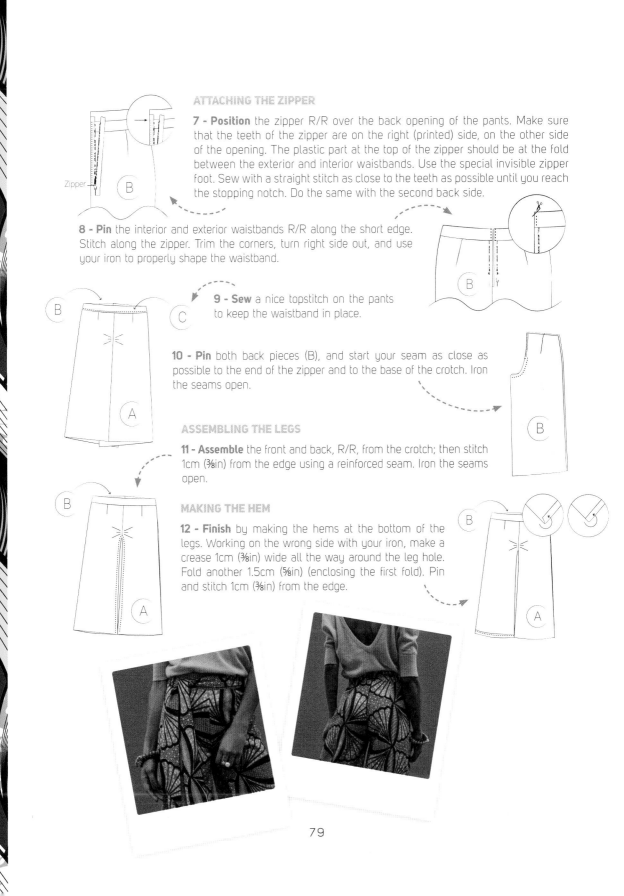

17

The Ben Pants

Ben: simple cropped pants—nicely tapered to highlight your legs, belt loops so you can dress them up with a belt, and that's it. A basic for any time of year.

Necessary Materials

For a size 16
- 210cm (2¼yds) (110cm/43⅜in width)
- Fusible interfacing to reinforce waistband
- 22cm (8¾in) invisible zipper in navy blue

For a size 24
- 220cm (2⅜yds) (110cm/43⅜in width)
- Fusible interfacing to reinforce waistband
- 22cm (8¾in) invisible zipper in navy blue

PATTERN

To access the pattern pieces through the QR code below, open the camera app on your phone, aim the camera at the QR code, and click the link that pops up on the screen.

To access the pattern through the tiny url, type the web address provided into your browser window.

tinyurl.com/11518-pattern17-download

SEAM ALLOWANCES
Seam allowances are not included. You will need to add 1cm (⅜in) on all sides of your pieces.

Cutting Layout

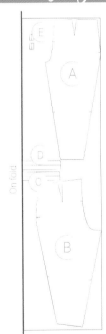

Instructions

MAKING THE DARTS

1 - Form the darts in the front (A) and back (B) pieces of the pants. To do this, bring the dart lines together R/R. Stitch on the wrong side of the fabric along the dart line. At the tip, do not stop, but continue a few more stitches off the fabric; then tie a knot to reinforce the dart closure. Iron down the inside of the darts.

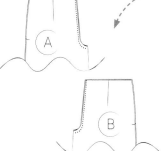

ASSEMBLING THE FRONT AND BACK

2 - Pin the front pieces (A) R/R; then assemble them from the crotch using a reinforced stitch. Use the notches to accurately position your pieces. Repeat with the back pieces (B).

3 - Assemble the previously prepared front and back pieces, edge to edge and R/R, along one side only (the zipper will go on the other side). Pin and stitch 1cm (⅜in) from the edge. Iron the seams open.

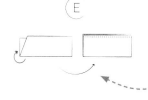

MAKING THE BELT LOOPS

4 - Fold the loop (E) R/R and lengthwise, and stitch 1cm (⅜in) from the edge along the longest edge. Turn the loop right side out, and press with an iron. Do the same for the other loops.

MAKING THE WAISTBAND

For the rest of the instructions, we will call "C'" and "D'" the "interior" front and back waistbands, respectively. Before starting, apply interfacing to the "exterior" front (C) and back (D) waistband pieces, which will be visible when the pants are worn.

5 - Pin the front (C) and back (D) waistbands together R/R along one side (the same side on which you previously assembled the pants). Stitch 1cm (⅜in) from the edge and iron the seams open. Repeat with the interior waistband.

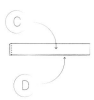

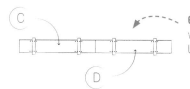

6 - Position the loops R/R on the front (C) and back (D) pieces of the exterior waistband, level with the notches. Stitch 3mm (⅛in) from the edge to keep the loops in place.

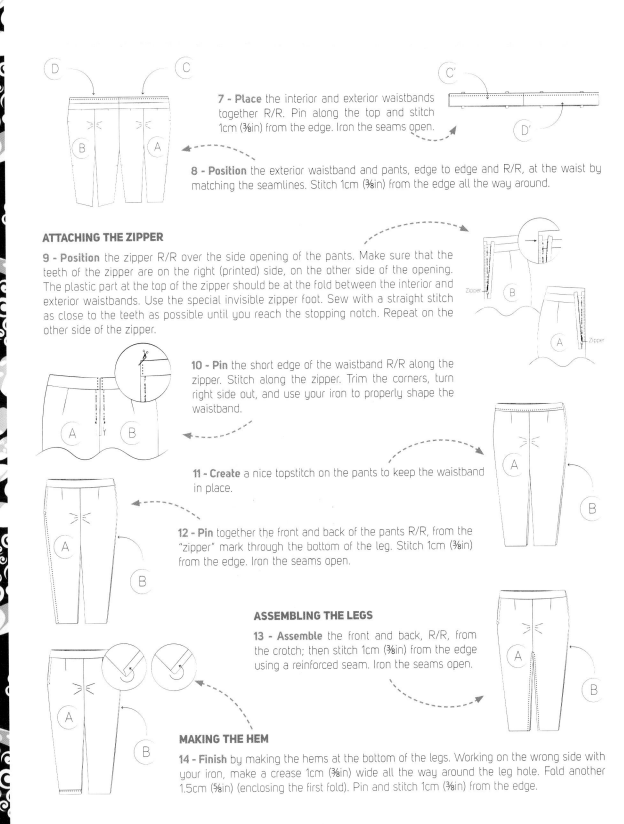

7 - Place the interior and exterior waistbands together R/R. Pin along the top and stitch 1cm (⅜in) from the edge. Iron the seams open.

8 - Position the exterior waistband and pants, edge to edge and R/R, at the waist by matching the seamlines. Stitch 1cm (⅜in) from the edge all the way around.

ATTACHING THE ZIPPER

9 - Position the zipper R/R over the side opening of the pants. Make sure that the teeth of the zipper are on the right (printed) side, on the other side of the opening. The plastic part at the top of the zipper should be at the fold between the interior and exterior waistbands. Use the special invisible zipper foot. Sew with a straight stitch as close to the teeth as possible until you reach the stopping notch. Repeat on the other side of the zipper.

10 - Pin the short edge of the waistband R/R along the zipper. Stitch along the zipper. Trim the corners, turn right side out, and use your iron to properly shape the waistband.

11 - Create a nice topstitch on the pants to keep the waistband in place.

12 - Pin together the front and back of the pants R/R, from the "zipper" mark through the bottom of the leg. Stitch 1cm (⅜in) from the edge. Iron the seams open.

ASSEMBLING THE LEGS

13 - Assemble the front and back, R/R, from the crotch; then stitch 1cm (⅜in) from the edge using a reinforced seam. Iron the seams open.

MAKING THE HEM

14 - Finish by making the hems at the bottom of the legs. Working on the wrong side with your iron, make a crease 1cm (⅜in) wide all the way around the leg hole. Fold another 1.5cm (⅝in) (enclosing the first fold). Pin and stitch 1cm (⅜in) from the edge.

18
The Anne-So
Clutch

Don't judge a book by its cover—Anne-So has more than one trick in the bag! Thanks to its folding system, Anne-So changes size and look in no time. A clutch for many occasions.

Necessary Materials

30cm (⅓yd) of fabric A (110cm/43⅜in width) • 30cm (⅓yd) of fabric B (110cm/43⅜in width) • 50cm (⅝yd) for lining • 80cm (⅞yd) of piping (optional) • 25cm (9⅞in) separating (open-ended) zipper in ecru

SEAM ALLOWANCES
Seam allowances are not included. You will need to add 1cm (⅜in) on all sides of your pieces.

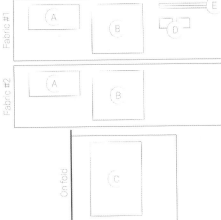

PATTERN
To access the pattern pieces through the QR code below, open the camera app on your phone, aim the camera at the QR code, and click the link that pops up on the screen.

To access the pattern through the tiny url, type the web address provided into your browser window.
tinyurl.com/11518-pattern18-download

Instructions

MAKING THE OUTER BAG

1 - Start by making your exterior fabric panels. To do this, position pieces A and B R/R, and pin them along a short edge. If you so choose, you can insert piping to add a touch of originality to your clutch. Repeat with the other two fabric panels. Iron the seams open.

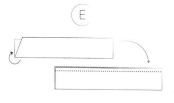

MAKING THE WRIST STRAP

2 - Fold the wrist strap (E) R/R lengthwise. Pin and stitch 1cm (⅜in) from the edge; then turn right side out.

PREPARING THE ZIPPER TABS

3 - Using your iron, crease the back of the zipper tab (D) 1cm (⅜in) from the edge on each side widthwise. Then fold it in half, edge to edge, still in the width direction. Crease well with your iron to keep in place.

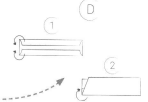

PREPARING THE ZIPPER

4 - Start by cutting off the excess fabric at the ends of the zipper. Use the zipper tab to enclose the ends of the zipper. They should come just over the metal parts located at the ends. Pin and stitch 5mm (³⁄₁₆in) from the edge. You may want to use the hand wheel on your sewing machine when you get close to the teeth to avoid breaking the needle.

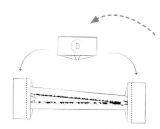

ATTACHING THE ZIPPER

5 - Position the zipper R/R on the previously assembled front piece (A). If the zipper tabs stick out a little, it's not a big deal. Lay one of the lining pieces (C) wrong side up (the exterior fabric and lining should be facing each other). Pin and stitch using the special zipper foot as close to the teeth as possible. Do the same with the other front panel and lining.

6 - Using your iron, press the seams to start shaping the clutch. If you so choose, you can topstitch along the zipper to keep it securely in place.

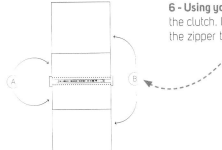

ASSEMBLING THE CLUTCH AND LINING

7 - To do this, unfold your "exterior" fabric and your "lining" fabrics on either side of the zipper, which should be slightly open.

10cm (4in)

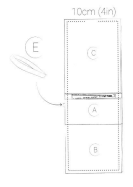

8 - Place the exterior panels R/R and sandwich the wrist strap between the two layers, about 4cm (1⅝in) below the zipper. Pin all the way around, folding the zipper tab toward the "exterior" fabric and accurately matching the sides. Continue by positioning the linings edge to edge and R/R. Stitch 1cm (⅜in) from the edge all the way around, leaving a 10cm (4in) opening at the bottom of the lining.

9 - Notch the corners, and turn the clutch right side out via the hole in the lining and the opening left in the zipper. Hand-sew the lining closed using an invisible stitch.

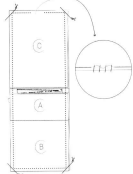

4 pieces

19
The Élo
Bag

Who said a bag should only be useful? Certainly not Élo, which combines practicality (with its ample space and two pockets) and originality, with its paneling and large handles that give structure to its style. The little bonus: Élo is fully lined!

Necessary Materials
- 125cm (1⅜yds) of fabric (110cm/43⅜in width) for a single fabric OR 40cm (½yd) of each fabric (Fabric #1, Fabric #2, and lining)
- 260cm (2¾yds) of strapping

SEAM ALLOWANCES
Seam allowances are not included. You will need to add 1cm (⅜in) on all sides of your pieces.

Cutting Layout

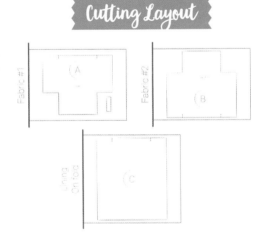

PATTERN
To access the pattern pieces through the QR code below, open the camera app on your phone, aim the camera at the QR code, and click the link that pops up on the screen.

To access the pattern through the tiny url, type the web address provided into your browser window.
tinyurl.com/11518-pattern19-download

ASSEMBLING THE OUTER FABRICS

1 - Place pieces A and B R/R, and pin them all the way around the edge (including pockets); then stitch 1cm (⅜in) from the edge.
Using your iron, fold the seams and the pocket down toward the bottom of the bag (in the direction of piece B).

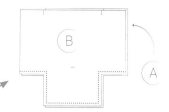

ASSEMBLING THE HANDLES

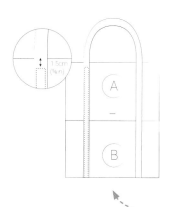

2 - Cut two 130cm (51¼in) lengths of strapping. Take one strap and place it on top of one of the previously assembled exterior panels. To position the straps correctly, start from the bottom of piece B and center it on the appropriate notch; then draw the strap up to the top of piece A, again centering it on the notch. Repeat with the other side of the strap. Be careful not to twist the straps when positioning them. Stitch 3mm (⅛in) from the edge all the way around the straps. Be aware that you need to stop sewing 1.5cm (⅝in) from the edge of the opening of your bag.
Repeat on the other side of the bag.

3 - Assemble the two previously prepared exterior "fabric" pieces R/R at the sides and bottom of the bag. Pin and stitch 1cm (⅜in) from the edge. Match the seams of the panels as well as the positioning of the straps at the bottom of the bag.

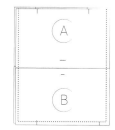

4 - Repeat with the lining, leaving at least a 10cm (4in) opening at the bottom of the lining.

5 - Give the bag a little volume by making a pleat at the bottom of the bag. To do this, layer the bottom seam of the bag with the side seam. A triangular shape is formed. Measure 3cm (1¼in) from the corner and draw a line perpendicular to the seam. Stitch on this line. Before turning right side out, trim the excess fabric.
Repeat with the previously assembled linings.

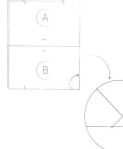

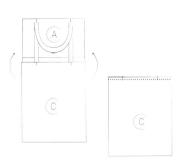

ASSEMBLING THE BAG AND LINING

6 - Slide the "outer" bag inside the lining, so that the bag and lining are R/R. The straps must be inside and therefore are no longer visible. Pin and stitch all the way around. Be sure to fold the straps toward the inside of the bag so as not to catch them in the seam.

7 - Turn right side out via the opening left in the lining. Hand sew it closed using an invisible stitch.

LEVEL 1/5

2 pieces

20 The Mélinda Headband

Mélinda is the basic headband that will enhance your hair and define your outfit!

Necessary Materials
- 30cm (⅓yd) of fabric (110cm/43⅜in width)
- 25cm (9⅞in) of 2cm (⅞in)-wide elastic

Cutting Layout

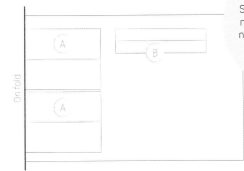

SEAM ALLOWANCES
Seam allowances are not included. You will need to add 1cm (⅜in) on all sides of your pieces.

PATTERN
To access the pattern pieces through the QR code below, open the camera app on your phone, aim the camera at the QR code, and click the link that pops up on the screen.

To access the pattern through the tiny url, type the web address provided into your browser window.
tinyurl.com/11518-pattern20-download

MAKING THE EXTERIOR FABRIC

1 - Fold pieces A in half, R/R, lengthwise. Pin the free side lengthwise and stitch 1cm (⅜in) from the edge.
Turn your pieces right side out. Do the same for the second piece A.

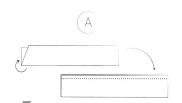

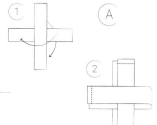

2 - Place the two strips on top of each other in an X and fold them over each other to form a link.
Pin the sides edge to edge and stitch 0.7cm (⅓in) from the edge.

MAKING THE ELASTIC BAND

3 - Fold piece B in half, R/R, lengthwise. Pin the free side and stitch 1cm (⅜in) from the edge. Turn the piece right side out.

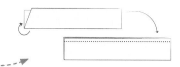

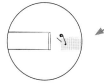

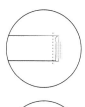

4 - Cut a piece of elastic to close your headband. To find out how long you need, take your tape measure and the fabric link previously assembled from your A pieces and wrap them around your head. Measure the remaining gap between the two fabric ends.
Attach a safety pin to the end of the elastic and slide it into the tube using piece B. Play with the fabric to move the safety pin through the tube.
When the other end (the one without the pin) is about to enter the tube, pin the elastic to the edge of the fabric and stitch 7mm (⅓in) from the edge with a reinforced stitch.
Continue to pull the safety pin through until the elastic reappears on the other side of the tube. When the elastic reappears on the other side, pin it and stitch 7mm (⅓in) from the edge with a reinforced stitch.

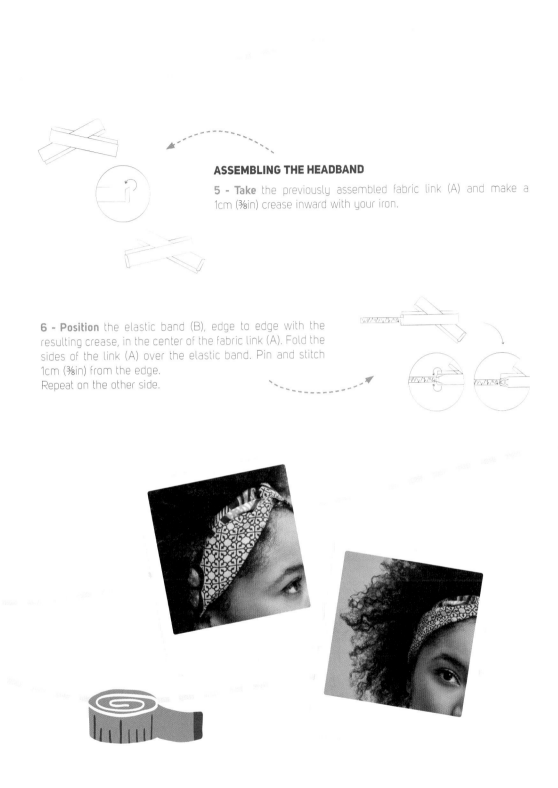

ASSEMBLING THE HEADBAND

5 - Take the previously assembled fabric link (A) and make a 1cm (⅜in) crease inward with your iron.

6 - Position the elastic band (B), edge to edge with the resulting crease, in the center of the fabric link (A). Fold the sides of the link (A) over the elastic band. Pin and stitch 1cm (⅜in) from the edge.
Repeat on the other side.

Imperial Conversions

The imperial measurements in this book follow standard conversion practices for sewing and soft crafts. The imperial equivalents are often rounded off for ease of use. If you need more exact measurements, there are a number of amazing online converters.

Creating with African Wax Fabric

First published in the United States in 2022 by Stash Books, an imprint of C&T Publishing, Inc., P.O. Box 1456, Lafayette, CA 94549

Coudre le wax! © 2021 by Éditions Marie Claire - Société d'Information et de Créations (SIC)

This edition of "*Coudre le wax!*" first published in France by Éditions Marie Claire in 2021 is published by arrangement with Marie Claire.

PUBLISHER: Amy Barrett-Daffin

CREATIVE DIRECTOR: Gailen Runge

ACQUISITIONS EDITOR: Roxane Cerda

EDITOR: Jennifer Warren

ENGLISH-LANGUAGE COVER DESIGNER: April Mostek

ENGLISH TRANSLATION: Kristy Darling Finder

PRODUCTION COORDINATOR: Zinnia Heinzmann

Printed in the USA

10 9 8 7 6 5 4 3 2 1